THE Jesus Lady

HEART TO HEART

JAN KNOTTS

© 2022 by Beacon Street Press. All rights reserved.
No part of this book may be used or reproduced in any manner whatsoever without written permission of the publisher.

For more information, contact:

BEACON STREET PRESS
500 Beacon Drive
Oklahoma City, OK 73127

1-800-652-1144
www.swrc.com

Printed in the United States of America

ISBN 978-1-933641-76-8

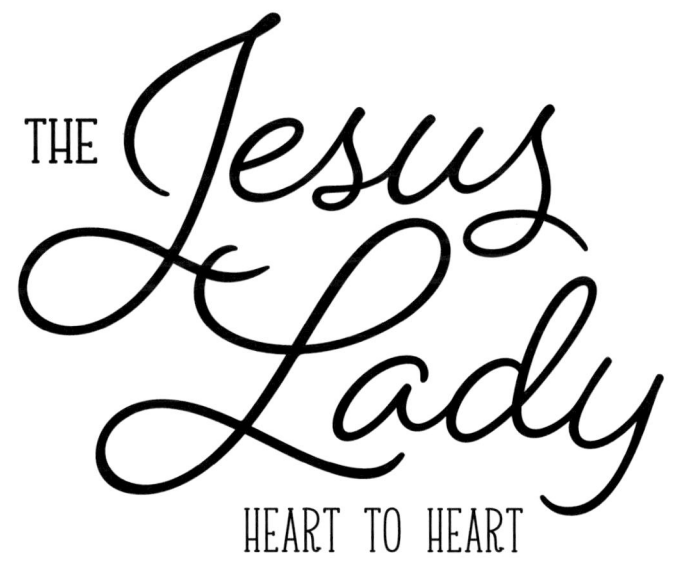

THE Jesus Lady
HEART TO HEART

Table of Contents

Prologue 1

Beginnings 7

Students 17

Photo Album 29

Lessons 37

Miracles 75

Closing 98

May I always reflect Jesus and Him alone.

May I always seek His will, not my want.

May the words of my mouth and the meditation of my heart be acceptable in Thy sight, my Lord, my rock and my redeemer.

Prologue

Imagine my surprise the day I realized that my great and mighty God had a plan for my life from the very beginning. His hand was on me even as a strong-willed little girl.

I was the second of six children. My older sister, Kitty, was so pretty in my eyes. I never thought I could measure up to her. Besides she was smart to boot. I was more than happy to be a little bookworm as I grew up. If I got any attention, it seemed to be negative. As a result, I hid in my room as much as possible.

But just like that, one day my whole life changed. I was in kindergarten at the time. I had an ongoing sore throat. After a visit to the doctor, I learned that I was going to have to go to the hospital to have my tonsils removed. I remember being in the same room as my mother who oddly enough had to have her tonsils removed as an adult.

My sweet teacher had the other students make me cards and she then brought them to the hospital for me. For the first time, I felt really special. All the attention all of a sudden was being showered down on me. The rest of that school year was an absolute joy because I finally fit right in.

Then came first grade. What a tragedy! I remember my teacher's name really well. It was Miss Gaffney. She remembered my name, as well. She no doubt hadn't received the memo on how special I really was. She treated me exactly like she treated everyone else. Now what was I supposed to do? I couldn't go back into the hospital. You can only do tonsils once. Right then and there, I decided I wouldn't do a thing for this teacher.

The day came that I really rebelled. I tore the belt off both sides of my pretty little cotton dress. I removed my shoes and socks and tied my feet together at the ankles. I tied them as tight as I possibly could. Miss Gaffney eventually called my name wanting me to go to the blackboard to do a simple math problem. I responded that I couldn't. She asked me why. I replied, "Because I can't walk," with all the attitude of a 6-year-old.

She had me stand up beside my desk and saw what I had done. She asked me why I did such a thing. I answered, "Because I hate you." YIKES. Miss Gaffney had me march my little barefooted self, right out the door. I can still hear in my mind the laughter from the rest of the kids as I went up the aisle and hopped across the front of the room on my way out the door.

I was told to sit on the bottom step of stairs that went to the second floor. The principal was called to cut off the ties because I had knotted them so tightly that they could neither one untie them. Then I followed the principal into her office. She realized eventually that I was rebellious because of this need for attention created by my kindergarten experience after talking to my mother.

I became the first and only first-grader to have detention every day after school. Each day I was required to sit quietly in my classroom seat while the other students did their worksheets and listened to the teacher. Then after they were dismissed to go home, I went to the principal's office. There I did the very same worksheets as they had done. After the principal checked my papers, she would give me a piece of chocolate candy and send me away. We only lived a block or so from the school.

I'd skip on down the block thinking how dumb the other kids were. They did worksheets for nothing. I got candy. I felt special and smart, too. What a deal.

After I was grown up with a son of my own, my mother called me to inform me that Miss Gaffney was in the hospital in town and doing really poorly. She asked how her star student was doing. She said she never forgot me. Understandable! I traveled the few hours to return to my small hometown to visit her one last time. It was a sweet experience for us both.

God was preparing me, I realize, to teach young children years later. In all my 30-plus years of teaching Bible classes to third-graders, I've never had a student as bad as I was. I was equipped to recognize a child who needed just a bit more love and attention than the others. I had been where they were. God was forming me into His likeness.

History of Joy El Camps

In 1938, Children's Bible Mission, also known as CBM, began. Miss Mildred McEvers was CBM's home missionary assigned to South Central Pennsylvania. She began teaching the Word of God to boys and girls in Franklin and Perry Counties in public schools.

In 1965, the U.S. Supreme Court declared it to be illegal to have Bible reading and prayer in public schools. Guided by the Lord in their effort to reach children, the local CBM Committee discovered that Pennsylvania had a law lying dormant, which permits students to be released from public school for the purpose of religious instruction.

With this knowledge, CBM developed what was then called the Released Time Bible Program, which allowed students to be released from their classrooms once a week for one hour to go to an offsite location to receive Bible teaching. Parents were required to turn in a signed permission slip if they wished their child to participate.

In 1967, Bible Released Time began in two elementary schools, The program met with favor with the parents, churches, the community and the students. Soon Bible Released Time became a familiar phrase.

From its inception, Bible Released Time included scripture memorization. To encourage students to memorize verses incentive awards were offered for various levels of points each student accumulated. The maximum award was a free week of summer camp. Initially CBM held its summer program in Greencastle, Pennsylvania. However, as more and more students earned free summer camp, CBM needed more weeks from the camp that they were renting, and began planning its own camping facility.

In 1974, groundbreaking was held at Camp Joy El on March 17. The first camp opened July 7 that same summer with a campground consisting of a dining hall/chapel building and 10 cabins. The camp facility was named Camp Joy El.

Over time Camp Joy El became the identity focus of the ministry and the name by which the whole of CBM Ministries was most widely known. Responding to that public perception in 2004 the Board of Directors took action to rename the entire organization "Joy El Ministries".

In recent years, because of the direction branding for marketing has taken, the ministry has created the "Joy El" brand with Joy El Generation, Joy El Camps and Retreats and has shortened the public name of the ministry to simply "Joy El"

Beginnings

Questions

Perhaps my mother thought I could be straightened out by attending the local Catholic school. For grades 3-5, the nuns tried their best. I had an unusual number of questions that needed to be answered. Once I asked how much time I would have to spend in Purgatory for telling a lie or talking back to my parents. They couldn't give me an answer.

My next question was, "By how much time could I shorten my punishment time in Purgatory each time I said the 'Our Father,' 'Hail Mary' or even the whole rosary." All they could respond with was, "I don't know. I don't know."

I knew I was misbehaving quite a lot but surely not enough to be walking around praying all the time like I was doing. I stated that I figured I'd be done praying and go on outside and play instead because I was wasting my life by praying so much.

I really wasn't all that bad. Was I? My Mother said that was backtalking to the nuns and not a good choice for me. I learned that if ever a child had a question, I'd better find an answer. Maybe I could save them a lot of grief if I could only find them the answer.

Eye-Opening Salvation

At the age of 32, on September 11, 1979, I received Jesus Christ as my personal Savior. My search for love and happiness was over. For some time, my mother had been asking me to pray for my older sister who was, in her words, involved in a cult. As a good little Catholic sister, I prayed that God would open her eyes and get her out of that cult.

Then in the summer of 1979, my sister, Kitty, returned with her family from Turkey where her husband had been stationed. He was in the Air Force and they had been overseas for a few years. Imagine my surprise when I laid eyes on her for the first time again. She literally glowed from within.

She explained that while there she had found the love of Jesus Christ personally. I wanted some of whatever made her so all-fired happy. I wanted to hear more about Jesus.

She told me of a book that a friend had given her to read while in Turkey. It was called "How to be a Winner." At the end of reading it, she accepted Christ. I wanted to read it. The book was in Ohio where they were to be stationed next. She promised she would send it. I waited and waited. I called her to ask if she'd sent it. She said she thought I was just being nice when I asked for it. Now she would really send it, and she did.

The book finally arrived. Upon finishing the book, I only had one burning question. How could I be saved?

I made the call to Ohio. My brother-in-law answered the call. Kitty was at a Bible study/prayer meeting. He asked if my call was important. I said only that I wanted to be saved. He called my sister. As only God could plan this timing, they were praying for me as the call came in. She hurried across the grass to her own home to call me back. She was crying too hard to pray with me. A speaker at their church by the name of Hayseed Stevens took the phone. He prayed with me to ask Jesus into my heart. The load that was lifted was tremendous. As I knelt alongside my bed, I was finally complete.

Here I was in the privacy of my own bedroom knowing I was anything but Catholic. I didn't know what I was, but I was done praying to Mary or any of the saints. My first question then was, "Where do I go to church now?"

We agreed that we should pray for God to show me where to go since they were all in Ohio. I had no idea what to look for. I prayed for God's direction. That week, a free paper came to my door, the kind that just has ads. BUT in the lower right-hand corner was a box that held scripture. The scripture was Proverbs 3:5-6: "Trust in the Lord with all your heart. Lean not on your own understanding. In all your ways acknowledge Him and He shall direct your path."

I thought that surely sounds like what I need. There was a phone number attached to the ad for a little church called Bethel Bible

Church. The call was answered by a sweet woman who happened to be the wife of the pastor. She asked what kind of church I was looking for. My answer was I had no idea except that I knew I wasn't Catholic anymore. Her husband had been a Catholic before being saved and becoming a Baptist pastor. Who better to answer every little question I had in my newfound faith?

Here Am I

Not too long after I was saved, I took my two children and drove to Ohio to visit my sister and her family. Sunday came around and we all went to her church. This became quite a memorable event.

The pastor's message included reading the scripture Isaiah 6:8: "Also I heard the voice of the Lord, saying, Who shall I send, and who will go for us? Then said I, Here am I; send me."

The pastor then asked if there was anyone in the church who could say that today. In all the fullness of my voice, I said "Here am I; send me."

Of course, I said it out loud. Needless to say, I got attention. My sister turned to me and whispered you really didn't have to say that out loud. I just thought if I really meant it, I should say it. Remember: I was pretty new to all this. How was I to know I should keep it to myself?

My God heard my voice and knew I sincerely meant it, and he began to mold me into what he wanted me to be. I began to learn how to be a servant. I learned how to be constantly aware of where I am and who God may have cross my path.

Romans 14:12: So then every one of us shall give account of himself to God.

My desire is to be what he wants me to be and go where he wants me to go to tell someone about him. My heart is humble and thankful whenever he chooses me to reach out to others with His love and compassion.

Beginning Bible Released Time

From Sept. 11, 1979, to April 24, 1982, I spent most of my time growing in the Lord. I wanted to know my Lord intimately. In about 1983, a woman named Mary Burns visited and sang in our church. I learned that her home was in Dillsburg as was mine. We talked for a while after the service was over. She shared that she was involved in a children's ministry called Bible Released Time.

I worked in the church's small Sunday school classes and always had a heart for children. At the age of 24, after I gave birth to my son, I said that I wanted another in nine months. His father died when he was just 6 months old. It was six years later that I gave birth to my daughter.

God only allowed me to have two. In His wisdom, he built for me a void that could be filled with many more children over the years—thousands actually.

I told Mary that I'd love to hear more about this program. I agreed to give it a try. Soon after, I visited our local little grocery store to hang a poster advertising our upcoming Vacation Bible School. The store owner, Bob Lehman said, "Let me tell you of a program for children you may be interested in. It is called Bible Released Time."

Before you know it, I was committed to work at two elementary schools because I couldn't say, "no," to either of these nice people.

The role of the listener in this program involves being placed with the same three students each week. We listen to them recite memorized verses. We pray with them and encourage them. My first two years, I worked as a listener. For 30 weeks of the school year, I got to love them as Jesus would have if he were here for that one hour a week.

The very first week that I sat with my new three little girls in Wellsville Elementary I saw God's wonderful hand so clearly. He had chosen to give me a little girl that I knew before she was even born.

Here's how that happened ... I was introduced to a young 17-year-old pregnant girl. Her child would turn out to be this precious little third-

Beginnings

grader named Teresa. I saw Teresa's last name and believed I knew her father. I told her she could ask him if he remembered my name.

In the past her father had been with my best friend. The next week, she came in with the news: He remembered me. He wanted to give me a call. I told her that was fine. He called and I shared Christ with him. He wasn't ready. His sweet little daughter was ready and accepted Christ in our third-grade class.

She and I have stayed in touch over the years. She is now 46. God has blessed me with having three of her daughters in my Bible Released Time classes. Each of her children accepted the Lord Jesus in my third-grade class.

Her oldest son actually was blessed with leading his own grandfather to the Lord before Teresa's dad — who wasn't ready to accept Christ years earlier — died.

When Teresa went to the hospital to give birth to her last child, my husband and I were honored to keep the four other children at our house for those days.

Becoming a Teacher

Being a listener was all I ever thought I wanted to do in Bible Released Time. God had other plans. In one of the elementary schools, I was a listener in a fifth-grade class. The teacher was absolutely the best. Not only was she a teacher in the public school but volunteered to teach in the Bible program, as well.

She even wrote a song for Bible Released Time called "Welcome to Released Time." It went like this:

> Welcome to Released Time
> We are happy to be here.
> Welcome to Released Time
> If you're glad just give a cheer.
> Sing along and make a joyful noise.
> We know Jesus loves all girls and boys.

> So, say your verses, praise His name
> And learn to love God's way.
> For this we know, He loves you so
> And He'll give you a bright new day.

This was sung to the tune of "Nothing is Impossible." She was so gifted.

One week she came to class and shared that she was facing throat surgery and needed someone to cover the class for her in her absence. She asked us to pray. I just love to pray so I did. The next week she asked if we'd prayed. Of course, I said, "Yes."

She asked if God had spoken to any of us. I knew I surely hadn't heard from Him. She then said, "Jan, I think you'd be really good at this. You should give it a try."

Who me? I was sure we weren't speaking to the same God. What in the world was she seeing that I wasn't? Here I was, the quiet observer. She asked me if I'd give it a try. Remember, I'm the one who hates to say, "no," to anybody.

So, the next week with great fear and trepidation, I got ready to teach her class. I just knew these fifth-graders were going to pick this bumbling idiot apart. Much to my surprise, as soon as I stepped to the front of the class, the greatest peace washed over me. In an instant I knew this was just what God wanted for me.

Talking about the love of my life, Jesus Christ, covered all my fears. I was lost in His shadow. All they saw was Him. He brought out a part of me that I didn't know he had put there. This was my spiritual gift. Who knew?

From that point on I was a teacher—for over 33 glorious years. Thousands of children have heard about Jesus and His love. I'm just a humble, unworthy servant that he has called into this ministry.

Before I knew it, I was teaching in all four of the elementary schools in our school district. In some of the schools, I taught third, fourth and fifth grades all together. Some years we averaged 100-plus students per week.

One year in Wellsville Elementary, we had all but one third-grader in our class held on Friday afternoon at the very end of the day. The teachers just loved having this time free to wrap up their week and have an empty classroom. The child that didn't have permission to attend was a Jehovah Witness. No matter how much the teacher wanted him to join all the other students walking on down the block to the church, it wasn't going to happen.

In this small church, we began with maybe 20 students in one small room. We grew to over 30 in a double-sized room sitting on the floor with a path down the middle. Eventually we were moved up to the sanctuary.

Moms Breakfasts

When I began as a teacher in Wellsville, I felt God could use me more effectively if I got to know the moms of my students a bit. That way, I could pray for these families better. I began to set up a breakfast date with a different student's mom every week at a local diner. They would share prayer concerns with me. Many became friends. Some just trusted me a bit more with their child since I was no longer a stranger to them.

Each year in the summer, I would plan a girls' sleepover at our big farm house. We'd eat popcorn, watch movies, play games, get wet from water balloons, and so on. It was super fun.

My husband and I would take the boys to our neighborhood state park to fish for the day in the lake from the bank. He had lots of hooks to bait. Only one parent ever had a problem with that.

One year, there were so many girls planning to come to the sleepover that we got permission to use our local Christian camp, called Kings Kids Camp. However, I got deathly sick and had to go home. Some of my now-grown-up past students and a parent or two came out and stayed at the camp to fill in for me because I needed to go home.

The next day I arrived to find cards and posters made by them—all for me. That was precious. That was far better even than my chocolate in first grade in the principal's office or my cards in kindergarten.

Northern York County School District

A few years into my teaching years with Bible Released Time it became necessary for me to seek a full-time job in order to have insurance benefits. This could have presented a major conflict since I was already working part time in the offices and as a teacher's aid.

Our local school district also conducted an annual door-to-door census each summer to pick up new residents for our school tax information. I found that I really enjoyed doing that. Talking to people was surely no longer a problem for me. The superintendent's secretary would give me another area as soon as I completed what she had given me previously. Others couldn't handle people who were rude to them. I, on the other hand, was challenged and kept being nice.

I went to the business manager and gave him an impossible proposition: I would do whatever job he created for me on the condition that I could work the following hours:

    Monday and Thursday – 6:30-4:00
    Wednesday – 6:30-9:00 and 12:00-4:00
    Tuesday and Friday – 6:30-12:00

That would enable me to work a total of 35 hours and receive benefits. It would also allow me to continue to teach in Bible Released Time on Tuesday and Friday afternoons.

Then I asked for God to do the absolute impossible. I requested to have off Wednesday mornings so I could continue attending a Bible study group from 9 to 12.

Standing firmly on Luke 1:37, "For with God, nothing shall be impossible," the business manager approached the board with my outlandish request. The school board accepted the offer.

Beginnings

The job included doing all of the census which involved visiting over 8,000 homes each year and working with the school district's seven tax collectors. These were both jobs that nobody was going to fight me for.

Actually no one even stepped in to do my job when I was on vacation.

I never even asked what my pay would be. Before my first pay, I was asked what pay I wanted. I, of course, said, "I'm just here for the benefits. Any pay is fine."

I started out at only $10,000 per year. I remained the lowest paid employee in the whole school district up until my retirement 20 years later. What other employee could say that they got paid to get exercise and a suntan each year – while the others had to sit in the office all day?

On occasion I was blessed with leading someone to Christ while doing my census duties, and the tax collectors became treasured friends to me. Who needed money when all these blessings were raining down on me?

One day I knocked on a door while doing census. The woman who answered invited me in. We talked a little. She inquired what I do with my life when I'm not working. She then heard all about Bible Released Time.

Unbeknownst to me she had been praying for God to show her how to use her time for him. When I knocked on her door, she knew he was bringing her the answer. She became a listener at that point. That's so God.

Students

Autograph

One of my most treasured memories from my third-grade class came from a young autograph-seeker.

The students are encouraged to carry their Bibles to the Released Time class from school each week. After one class in particular, many students accepted Jesus into their hearts.

One little boy asked me afterward if I would sign his Bible. I didn't know I was famous. This surely wasn't about me. I intended to just put my name and phone number in his Bible so he could call anytime he might have questions.

The Bible he handed me was a Watchtower Jehovah Witnesses Bible. With a smile, I signed it. He then received a King James Bible. His parents contacted me shortly after.

James not only remained in our class, but later, his parents accepted Christ, as well. We have remained friends over many years. God had a bigger plan.

Louie

One young man named Louie was in my third-grade class one year. He was very attentive. From an unchurched family, one fine day, he asked Jesus to come into his heart. Then as a result, his whole family came to accept Christ. His sister was later in my class and was saved.

His family has long been a remarkable example of fine Christians.

Did I mention that Louie is now the youth pastor at the very church he accepted Christ in, about 40 years ago? He is leading other children to the Lord and training them up in the way they should go.

God has kept the blessings rolling right along. His sons have been in our class, probably sitting in the very same seat that their dad occupied many years ago. The story goes on and on and on...

Jason

Some would say there is a law requiring a separation between church and state. I'm here to say that there is no such law in the eyes of God. One year, after teaching the students about the fall of man and God's answer to our sin, many accepted Jesus.

God chose to draw one little boy near a few days later. While I was working as an aide on the playground, Jason approached me with a request. He wanted me to pray with him to ask Jesus into his heart right there on the elementary school playground.

We were surrounded by other boys and girls as well as a few other aides. I envisioned being fired on the spot. So, I said, "Jason, can't you wait until Tuesday when we are at Bible Released Time?"

I shouldn't have been surprised as he answered "No. I want to do it now. I waited since last night and I want to pray now."

About that time, another student fell and got a bloody nose. I saw that as the hand of God. I jumped at the chance to tell Jason I needed to take that little boy to the nurse's office and we would have to wait until Tuesday to pray. God had given me an out and kept me employed for another day.

That should have been the end of it, or so I thought. While I was in the nurse's office the bell rang to end recess. Imagine my surprise when I came out of the nurse's office and there stood Jason. He was waiting just outside the door to the nurse's office in the hallway.

His words will remain with me forever. "Can we pray now? I waited."

Then I realized God had bigger plans than I had foreseen. Jason and I went around the corner from the office in the hallway and held hands and prayed. Right there in the hallway of the elementary school, he accepted Christ as his Savior. If I had been fired right then and there, God would have led me to another job.

His parents and I met through the census. Later on, I got to pray with both of them. They lived just a block up the street from the administrative office where I worked each day.

Once a year our little town of Dillsburg has a festivity called Farmers' Fair. Each year, I was invited to Jason's house to fix a plate of food and enjoy the parade that passed by their house. Jason, his mom and dad are all in Heaven now, but the precious memory of that family will remain with me forever.

Now and then, a teacher gets tired enough that Satan tries to convince her that she just needs a night off. One evening, we at Bible Released Time planned to have a special program, presented by the older students, for all the students and their parents. The third-graders would just be part of the audience.

It didn't even seem necessary that I be there. "Really, I could use a little down time," I said to myself. This would be a good time to just stay at home and rest under a big fluffy blanket. Who would miss me anyway? No Big Deal!

But God prompted me to go and sit in the audience with my third-graders and watch. My plan was to sit in the very back and quietly observe. I sat in the last row just like I'd planned.

The next thing I knew, Sasha came back and slid into the row beside me. She said she was very glad to see me because she wanted to ask Jesus into her heart. "Could we please pray now?"

"Why, of course." Whenever the Holy Spirit moves in a child's life, we must be ready. He has no fixed schedules. He moves whenever he's ready.

Somehow, I may have forgotten to mention that when the students arrive at Bible Released Time, the first thing that they must do is put on a name badge so we can learn their names. This also helps us to see what students may be absent.

The Jesus Lady

One day, a young boy came into class visibly upset. When I asked him what was wrong, he replied, "Last night my hamster died." I reassured him that the Bible says animals will be in Heaven. After all, one day Jesus will come back riding on a white horse. Many others will be following behind him on horses as well.

I told him that I believed that our loved pets would be in Heaven not because they had asked Jesus into their heart but because we love them so much. God wants to give us the desires of our heart. For that reason, I believe our pets are in Heaven.

I said, "Marshall, I want you to picture your hamster in the hands of Jesus. When you get to Heaven, God will put your little hamster into your hands. Whenever I get to Heaven will you show me which hamster is yours?"

With all the innocence of a third-grader, he replied, "Mrs. Knotts, you'll know him. He'll have his name tag on."

Oh, silly me. What was I thinking?

Jean Luc

After a wonderful teaching unit on salvation where many boys and girls responded to the Gospel, I decided to follow up with a question the following week. I asked the students who now belonged to Jesus if they noticed anything different. One special student showed me the depth of his decision when he responded. He said that now when he prays, there's a tear.

May we as adults feel His presence as deeply as this young man! Whoever says children can't really understand the gospel has never come across a Jean Luc. Praise the Lord.

Hurting Child

Some children come from troubled families. A few young girls with a cutting problem have been in my class. Unable to handle stress, they reverted to hurting themselves.

Students

One day a listener approached me to let me know that one of her girls had been cutting herself and said she wanted to die. I asked the little girl if she would let me pray with her. She allowed me to pray.

I gave her a picture of a baby lamb in the arms of our loving shepherd. The picture showed clearly His nail-pierced hands. We talked about the picture. She allowed me to lead her to Christ.

I turned the picture over and wrote the day's date on the back with these instructions: Next time Satan tries to tell you to cut or that nobody loves you, tell him to get lost. He is a liar. On this very date you crawled into the loving arms of Jesus and you belong to Him, now and forever.

She went home a changed child. Sometime afterward, her mother died of a drug overdose, but she knew she could lean into Jesus.

Another year, a fifth-grader had a problem with cutting. She also had family problems. We spent a lot of time reassuring her of the love of the Lord. She accepted Christ, but her home life was still unstable.

Katie and I stayed in touch all through her middle and high school years, and her high school guidance counselor and I kept each other informed on her progress or lack thereof. During high school, she would sometimes call me at night if she was in a compromising situation. We became and remained friends over the years.

She got married and had children of her own. She still lives in our little town. Each year when Farmers' Fair has its parade, Katie could be counted on to find me at my usual spot along the road. We'd catch up and I would get to see her children.

Now an accomplished woman, she is precious to me. God has won. She has victory in Jesus.

Lindsay

Not so long ago, I had a third-grade little girl who said she was hearing voices telling her that she needed to die. She was wanting to hurt herself because of the voices. I contacted her dad. He said he was aware of her hearing voices.

One wonderful day, she accepted Jesus, but she was still tormented. After work one day, I decided to drive to her home, and while there I met her grandfather who also lived there. Lindsay wasn't home from school yet, so we talked.

He was a Catholic who wanted to understand a little more about what Lindsay was being taught. Before I left, he prayed with me to be saved. God often has a plan that is so much bigger than we can even imagine. We continue to be friends with Lindsay, her dad and her grandfather.

Answered Prayer

My goal as a teacher has always been to stress how much Jesus loves each of the boys and girls. I want them to also learn that God always hears their prayers. Hebrews 13:5 states clearly, "For he hath said, I will never leave thee or forsake thee."

Often, I encourage the children to look for answered prayer in their lives. One week, I asked if any of them had seen God answer a prayer for them. One little girl said God had answered a prayer for her. Her mom's boyfriend fought with her mom, and he threw both her and her mom out in the cold night and locked the door. She prayed that God would help them get back inside where it was warm. Later, the boyfriend told them to come back in. She was sent up to her bedroom where it was warm. It broke my heart, but to her, her prayer was answered.

Another time, a little boy asked for prayer that his mother's boyfriend wouldn't get out of prison and come to the house before he and his mom got moved out. Within months, they had moved out. I have no

Students

idea if it was before the boyfriend returned or not. We have no idea how much time we have with these children. Only God knows, but may we be constantly vigilant.

Marriages

A true joy is watching students grow up and begin their own lives. Once, while going door-to-door for the census, a man opened the door and when I asked his name, he said, "Mrs. Knotts, you know me." He said I was his teacher in third-grade Bible Released Time. Of course, he had to give me his name, since I surely couldn't figure that one out.

There was a boy and girl who fell in love and got married. Can you imagine true love in elementary school? Years later, they invited me to the baby shower for their little boy. They are now fine parents of a son following in their footsteps in Bible Released Time.

Another successful life story is Rhonda. She is now a missionary in a foreign country and has been for many years. The Word of God goes forth and our God allows us to play some small part in furthering His kingdom.

Playground Evangelists

At Dillsburg Elementary School, we had a group of boys who were so excited about sharing the Gospel that they began their own playground outreach. They were quite exceptional. We kept seeing more and more boys coming to our classes. It seems that these boys were meeting on the playground at recess to help one another memorize their verses.

Before we knew it, other kids wanted to know what they were doing and were invited to join the group. Finally, they were praying for one another along with learning verses. They would then invite these new students to Bible Released Time, telling them what they were missing.

The high school may have "See you at the pole," but the elementary school has "See you on the playground." I am so curious to know what the Lord is doing in the lives of these young men now that they are adults!

One year, at South Mountain Elementary School, we had the most Spirit-filled students ever. They fervently prayed for one another and loved on each other. They helped each other with verses, and when we sang, it was beautiful. They would make a circle and hold hands, then they would raise their hands in praise for the Lord and sing. I'm sure it didn't sit well with Satan.

After that year, the Bible Released Time program for that school had to close for about two years because our staff was no longer available for a number of reasons. That was a heart-breaker. The Holy Spirit was truly evident in the students that were part of that group.

Heart Necklace

More than anything, I wish I could remember the name of a little third-grader I had in Wellsville one year. She gave me the most precious gift I've ever received from a student. As a matter of fact, I still have it with me in Florida where I'm living now.

After praying to ask Jesus into her heart, she made this gift for me—a necklace of many different colored beads on a string. What makes this especially wonderful is that on this string is also a pretty pink heart.

As she put it in my hand, she said, "I made this last night right after I prayed with my Daddy to ask Jesus into his heart."

That's why she put the heart on the necklace so I would always remember the night her Daddy gave his heart to Jesus. I just wanted to cry. God allowed me to play a small part in His plan in their lives, then he gave me the most precious souvenir.

It still hangs in my bedroom here, as it had hung in my bedroom in Pennsylvania ever since I received it.

John

After every three lessons in Bible Released Time, we have a review week. On that week, we have some kind of the game to see how much the students remember. We have played tic tac toe, jeopardy, and many others.

One such week, when I went to split the class into two teams, I realized I was short on one team. I had a problem. One of the listeners had her teenage son with her to assist in listening to the students' verses. I volunteered John to balance out the teams.

Here was the problem: John was heads taller than the students. When a team player answered a question correctly, he had to dash to the end of the room and back before anyone else. I thought it only fair to ask John to run backward.

I'm sure you can see where this could go wrong. On his return run backward, he tripped and fell. We allowed him to sit out the rest of the game.

The following week, he arrived with his arm in a cast. He broke his arm when he fell. I promised his poor mom that I wouldn't volunteer him in the future. Lesson learned.

Socks

One year, I needed surgery on my foot. It was very painful to wear shoes on it. When the boys and girls would arrive for class, I would remove my shoes. We'd sit on the floor in the sanctuary in our sock covered feet, shoes off.

They couldn't see any reason why I didn't need mine on but they did. For the longest time we had class that way. After a while they began to come to class wearing two different socks just to make the others laugh. After all the giggling stopped, the lesson would then begin. What sweet memories.

Old Friends

Some of the best friendships in the world have their roots in the Bible Released Time adults. Before the arrival of the students each week we would have a staff meeting. There we learned everything we needed to know about that class, card marking, upcoming events, etc. someone would share a devotional. Prayer needs were shared. We would pray for the kids and one another. A number of adults would walk the block or so up to the school for the boys and girls. Those who remained would join hands in a circle and pray for one another and share our burdens. These sweet people knew our hearts often better than our families. We were of one accord in our love of Christ and each other. I love these people more than words can express. We are truly part of one wonderful body. My lessons were prayed for each week before they were taught. The reason why so many children came to Christ is because of James 5:16; "The effectual fervent prayer of the righteous man avails much."

Photo Album

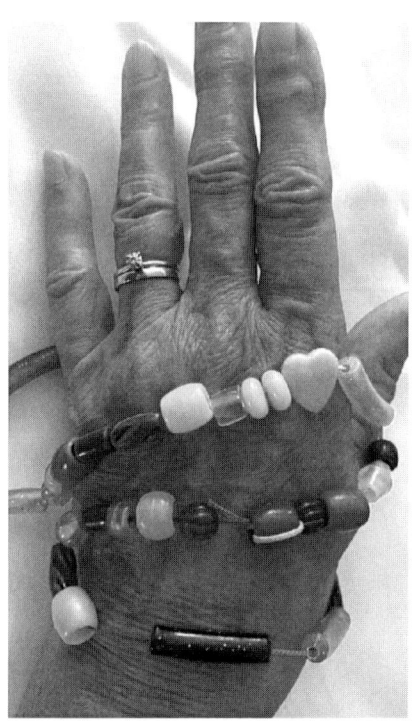

The Heart Necklace

Louie and Family

Shepherd Lamb Print

Alicia and Quinten

Annual Sleepover

Annual Fishing Adventure

Boys Praising the Lord

Boys Skating Party

Camp Joy El Week

Cathy and Caroline Leaders

Christmas Sweatshirt

Christmas Gift from God

Chuck Rhodes Visit

Photo Album

Girls Singing Praises

Fellow workers with Judy

End of Year Photo

Free Camp Awards Article

Game Time in Wellsville

The Jesus Lady

ME UPDATE
"What joy unspeakable"
by Jan Knotts

On a warm summer evening 1979, I asked the Lord Jesus to :come my personal Savior and ive Him complete control of my '. I had no way of knowing ere He would lead me but iimed Proverbs 3:5-6 to mory to be assured of His di- ion for my path. As He opened ors for me to serve Him, I anxiously entered. Go wed me to find more joy than ever imagined i four years through Bible Released Time.

ter the first year as a listener in Wellsville and Dill ols, I began to teach third graders in both sc t a blessing! This year when a coordinato ded, I felt God leading me to try to serve Him i as well. Now, not only was I blessed by a clos my third graders, but with the other students a est family of Released Time volunteers that have imagined. God has opened doors for His work in the overnight ministry at Camp Jo ver the past few years. He has blessed my li able to share Him with His children from districts and see them accept Him as their joy unspeakable.

eart overflows with love for my Lord and c us lives He's placed around me. Truly m ws as I watch all the bread being cast u coming back multiplied.

esire is to teach God's children to love the L r heart and live each day as His instrument

along with her volunteers, have a vital min ldren of Dillsburg elementary school

My Humble Beginning

Girls Skating Party

Home Schooled Sisters

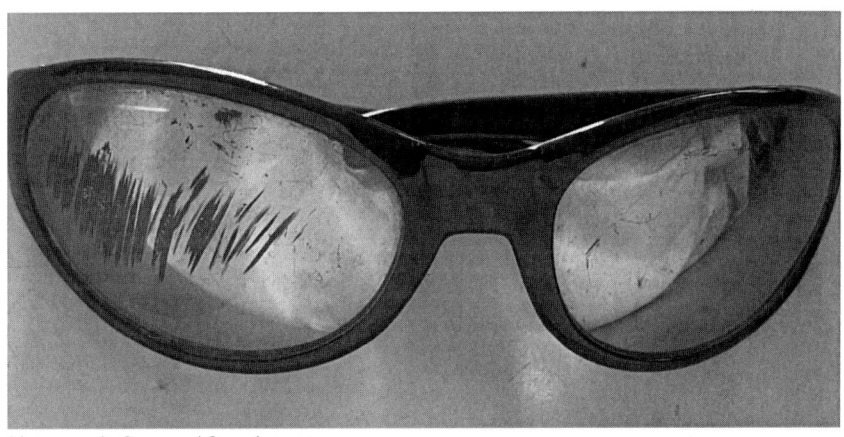

Motorcycle Scraped Sunglasses

Photo Album

Newspaper Celebrity Visit

Rose and Sue, Long Time Leaders

Student Receiving Award

Student Teaching Class

Student Teaching Class

The Jesus Lady

Student Teaching Class

Sword Drill Find That Verse

Students with Earned Rewards and Listeners

Sword Drill Bibles Up

Students Skit

Photo Album

35

Teaching at Wellsville

What's Next Money Order

Theresa, Former 3rd Grade Student

Annual Sleepover

Volunteer Pastors, Now in Heaven

Fellow Servants and Friends

Lessons

Memorization

The goal of Bible Released Time has always been to reach a child for the Lord and then teach them to love God's Word. Scripture memorization is vitally important. They learn that is their most powerful weapon against the devil as they travel through this life.

They must memorize the Bible verses at home before they arrive at class. Listeners may help with each verse only one time. This help is called "a prompting." It consists of either the scripture address of the verse or three consecutive words. It can't be both but just one or the other.

The staff has a great time acting out a skit to teach them how that works. Visuals work so much better than just telling them. This skit is acted out on one of the first classes of each school year. It consists of a listener and three students (all played by adults).

The listener hands each student a verse card to hold with the three verses they may say for that unit of lessons. They have this one opportunity to refresh their memory. The listener turns to the first student and has them turn their verse card face down on their lap since it will be their turn to recite first. Then it plays out like this:

Teacher:	Now (student A) it's your turn to recite what you've learned.
A:	John 3:16 I need help.
Teacher:	For God so … Now it's your turn.
A:	For God so loved the world …I need a little more help
Teacher:	I'm sorry but you've already had your help for this verse. Do you have another verse?
A:	No that's all I had for today.
Teacher:	Well, you can either do a worksheet or study your verses for next week

(Teacher turns to student B)

B: I'm ready. John 3:16 – For God so loved the world that he gave His only begotten son, that whosoever believeth in him should not perish but have everlasting life.

Teacher: Good job. Do you have another?

B: Yes. Romans 3:23 – For all have sinned and come short of the glory of God.

Teacher: Wow. You've earned two points. Can you say the third?

B: I think so. Romans 6:23 – Can you help me?

Teacher: For the wages ...

B: For the wages of sin is death; but the gift of God is eternal life through Jesus Christ our Lord. I even learned a bonus verse. Psalms 23:1 – The Lord is my shepherd I shall not want.

Teacher: Great job. Today you've earned 4 points. Keep up the good work.

C: I know Romans 3:23 – For all have sinned and come short of the glory of God. I learned a bonus verse too. Psalms 23:1 – The Lord is my shepherd I shall not want. I think that's all for today.

Teacher: You've earned two points for today. Good job.

This skit helps the students to visualize what it means to have just one help (or prompting) per verse. Besides memorizing the verses, students can earn points for looking up the verse in their Bible and explaining what the verse means.

Meanings are taught in class time so that they are not just memorizing words but are understanding what God wants them to take away from that verse.

Students

Skit on Prayer

We acted out another skit to illustrate the necessity of giving God our total attention when we pray. The students learned the importance of closing their eyes when praying and how distracted a person could be if they tried to pray while looking around.

This is a vitally important lesson to learn especially when the time comes when students ask the Lord Jesus to come into their hearts. Their choice must be private.

At the conclusion of each lesson, children are given an invitation to accept Christ. I have all the students close their eyes and keep them closed until they hear "Amen."

A prayer similar to this is prayed: "God I know that I have sinned. I'm sorry. I know I deserve to be punished. I believe that Jesus took my punishment for me. I believe he died in my place and rose from the dead three days later. Right now, I believe he's in Heaven preparing a place for me. I ask you, Jesus, to come into my heart and remove all my sins."

> Romans 10:9: That if thou shalt confess with thy mouth the Lord Jesus, and shalt believe in thine heart that God hath raised him from the dead, thou shalt be saved.

The children are told to keep their eyes closed, because this is a private choice between a boy or girl and God alone. If they prayed that quietly in their mind, they are asked to raise their hand. That way, only the adults in the room see who has trusted Christ. The listeners then mark the date on the student's verse card. The secretary then sends the child's name to Camp Joy El. Joy El then sends a new birth certificate to the child's home as they have just become a Child of God.

In the skit, an adult sits with me and tells me about all her troubles, what a terrible day she is having. All the while she is talking, I am looking all around. I'm checking my hair and nails. I may look at the clock and appear bored. Never once do I pay any attention to her. She sees that I'm really not listening to her at all. Then I ask the students what this person must feel like when I ignore her.

They get it. They realize that is how God feels when we are so busy minding everyone else's business rather than giving him all of our attention. We need to love him enough to give him ONLY all our attention. As a result, the children become very quiet and attentive during prayer.

Bubble Gum

Whenever possible, share something from your own life as a child to convey to the children that you really understand what they feel as a child. This helps them realize that you are not perfect. They should know that no one is. I've shared a story from my past that later has been shared with their parents, who then know I wasn't perfect, as well.

The story goes like this. My best girlfriend and I walked to a little neighborhood store that sold penny candy. It was called a 5 & 10 cent store. We sure don't have those anymore. On my nightstand stood an empty bubble gum machine. The bubble gum balls had been gone for a long time. When it was new it was full. When you put in a coin and slid a handle to the side, a bubble gum ball would fall out.

This way, I could save coins and have bubble gum, too. Now it was useless. It was empty. All I wanted was a few colorful bubble gum balls to put in it. On a shelf sat a small box of colorful bubble gum balls. Now, remember that I only wanted a few. I took down the box and opened the end. Then I learned a hard lesson.

> Exodus 20:15: Thou shalt not steal.

God in His own loving way caused the box of bubble gum balls to fall from my hands and bounce all over the floor. BOING, BOING, BOING!

Like a flash, the store owner came around the corner to see what all the racket was. There I stood, guilty. The last thing I heard as Carol

Lessons

and I dashed for the door was the voice of the store owner, "I know who you are. I know your mother."

I just knew that I was dead. Well, I was wrong. I was punished for sure. Now, I see that God loved me so much that he helped me learn a lesson the very first time I stole so that I'd never try it again. God sees everything we do.

One-Room Schoolhouse

In our little town of Dillsburg, we have a one-room schoolhouse. During the first month or so of each new school year, the third-, fourth- and fifth-graders get a tour of the building during what is called Heritage Days. They even get to sit in the old-time desks.

My friend Rose works at this schoolhouse and plays the part of an old-time teacher. Now, I didn't call her old, just the part she plays. On the wall of the classroom hangs a sign explaining punishments earned by various misbehaviors. Each act resulted in a number of lashes or smacks of the paddle.

The rules that were punishable were things such as:

Boys and girls playing together

Fighting at school

Quarreling at school

Gambling or betting at school

Playing cards at school

Climbing for every foot over three feet up a tree

Telling lies

Telling tales out of school

Giving each other ill names

Swearing at school

Misbehaving to girls

Drinking spiritous liquors at school

Making swings and swinging on them

Wearing long fingernails

Misbehaving to persons on the road

Going to girls' play places

Going to boys' play places

Coming to school with dirty faces and hands

Calling each other liars

Wrestling at school

Wetting each other washing at playtime

Scuffling at school

Going and playing about the mill or creek

Going about the barn or doing any mischief about the place

Can you imagine having rules such as these in our schools today? How simple times were back then.

Knowing they had experienced this tour, I created a story they could relate to. It goes like this:

In this one room schoolhouse, grades 1-8 attended together to be taught by the same teacher. Rules were very important to keep order in the class. Each day, the boys and girls would arrive in the morning. When the doors were opened, they were expected to hang their coats on the hooks in the cloakroom and put their lunch bags on the shelf above. When it was time for lunch, the teacher would dismiss them to get their lunches and sit at their desks to eat. One day at lunch time, a boy stated that his lunch bag was missing. The teacher asked the students who may have taken it. No one replied. The teacher had the students sit still until someone confessed. They were all hungry. It was so quiet in the room. Finally, a little boy, in second grade spoke up in a timid voice and said, "Teacher, I took the lunch."

His name was Tommy. Tommy was always such a good boy. The teacher asked why he would do that. Tommy said there was no food in their house for his mom to pack for his lunch. He had come without a lunch and was so very hungry. He thought he might just take a little bit out of the bag for himself. The teacher pointed out that was stealing, and he would need to get three smacks with the paddle.

Lessons

Tommy was instructed to walk up to her desk and place both of his hands on her desk and bend over. She went to the hook on the wall to remove the paddle. Just as she was ready to strike Tommy the first time, an older boy named David raised his hand with a strange request. He asked the teacher if she would allow him (David) to take the smacks for Tommy instead. The teacher said that has never happened before but she guessed that would be OK. Punishment was necessary after all.

So, David went to the desk and bent over top of Tommy, placing his hands over the smaller hands of Tommy. The teacher brought the paddle down. SMACK (smack the table one time), SMACK (smack the table one more time), SMACK (smack the table a third time). Then, the teacher told the boys they could again take their seats.

The students are by then visibly hurting and in the moment. Then, I ask how they think Tommy felt. Various answers were shared: sad, relieved, happy. That was exactly what Jesus did for each one of us, I explain. Jesus had done absolutely nothing wrong his entire life but he was beaten and then died because of sin that we have done.

> Isaiah 53:5: But he was wounded for our transgressions, he was bruised for our iniquities; the chastisement of our peace was upon Him; and with His stripes we are healed.

Almost always after this lesson, boys and girls are ready to put their faith in Jesus Christ and pray to be saved.

New Girl in Class

Role-playing is so effective. Another lesson that the boys and girls really relate to is the pretend story of the new girl in school. So many of them have had to be that new student in a new school district. In their short lives some of them have moved a number of times.

So, I pretend to be a new little girl that is sitting in their lunchroom on my very first day at school. This new girl is quiet and angry inside. Her parents had been having fights for quite a while. Finally, her Daddy left them and her mom decided to move them to this new place where daddy wouldn't find them anymore. The girl is missing her dad and all the friends she had in the old town she came from.

So here she sits all alone in the lunchroom. You see her. You know that Jesus loves her, but she doesn't seem to know that or she wouldn't seem so sad. Can you go up to her and say anything to help her? Could you share with her the love of Jesus?

But she says, "I won't ever believe that he loves me. How do you know?"

Student: "The Bible tells me so."

New girl: "That's just words in a book. How do you know it's even true?"

Student: "Because God can't lie. Jesus will never leave you."

New girl: "Well, my Daddy did. I never thought he would leave me."

Students will share their faith in Jesus to this poor new girl. In one class, we were so very caught up in the plight of this little girl that a third-grade little boy put his arms around me. He gave me a hug and said, "I will be your friend. I will never leave you."

I was so touched with his tender heart. He was so in the moment that he forgot I was his teacher. Imaginations are at their peak during those tender years. Their love is so pure and innocent. It's no wonder God says we are to come to him as little children.

> *Matthew 19:14: But Jesus said, Suffer the little children, and forbid them not, to come unto me: for of such is the kingdom of heaven.*

Christmas Sweatshirt

Each year I return to the Bible Released Time classroom to share the most exciting real-life Christmas story. I have shared this story for the last 30 years — in Sunday school classes; my large church in York, Pa.; various Bible studies; and my tiny church here in Florida.

I am humbled to realize that God chose to show His presence in my very ordinary life. It all begins on a Christmas Day so long ago. On Christmas Eve, we had our normal large family gathering. We had a feast and exchanged gifts with our children, grandchildren and great grandchildren and all their kin. We planned to leave early the following morning to begin to drive from Pennsylvania to Florida to spend some time with my husband's mother and brothers.

When I tell this story, I wear a red Christmas sweatshirt that has a picture of a white lamb and a black lamb on it. The lambs had on pretty little red and green scarfs. Across the bottom of the shirt, it quotes:

> *Isaiah 1:18: Though your sins be as scarlet, they shall be as white as snow.*

Early on Christmas morning, I put on that red sweatshirt, just hoping since it looks so Christmas-like that I might have an opportunity to share Christ with someone. It would be my ice-breaker.

My husband took the first part of the drive. After a few hours he asked if I wanted to take over. I was ready. I had only been driving a short distance when ahead of us we saw a big cloud of dust and dirt. It had been raining earlier. A car had slid off the road on its roof. Paul said we should pull over and see if we could be of any assistance.

Don't you know that Satan was shouting loudly within my head all the reasons why this was a bad idea. I'm not a nurse. I hate the sight of blood. I might pass out.

Then came the quiet voice of my God saying, "Didn't you wear this very sweatshirt hoping that you could tell someone about Jesus?"

So, we got out of the car and approached the car ahead of us on its roof. Another man, who had stopped right behind us, helped my husband cut the seat belt that held up this sweet woman. As soon as they cut the belt, she fell onto the roof. That sounds really funny but that's what she did.

They pulled her out onto the wet grass at my feet. Of course, she had a really big knot on her forehead that was bleeding. I tried not to look. She was a black woman a bit younger than I was. I asked her if she could tell me her name. "Thelma," she replied.

She could see my sweatshirt as I knelt by her head and commented on it. I asked Thelma if she died tonight, did she know if she would go to Heaven. Did she remember a time she asked Jesus to be her Lord and Savior? She replied, "Yes, honey, I have."

Of course, I asked God what in the world did I need to have stopped for, then? As I was questioning my presence, I noticed that another young woman had come up to us. She became my new best friend. She was a nurse on her way home from work. She immediately placed her hand on Thelma's head. I couldn't see it bleeding anymore. Thank you, Jesus.

I noticed the Christmas sweatshirt that this nurse had on. Thelma couldn't see it since the nurse was above Therma's head, so, I described it. It was white and had on it three angels. One was black. One was white and one was yellow. Under the angels were the words Peace on Earth.

I told Thelma she would like that shirt too. Thelma wanted me to pray for her husband and grandson who were still in the car being rescued as we were with her. I prayed with Thelma until the ambulance took them away.

My husband and I then got back in the car to head to Florida. We spent the night in South Carolina which was about halfway. The next morning, we finished driving the rest of the way. We arrived at Paul's family's home later that day, after Christmas.

After the family meal we all gathered to exchange gifts just as we had in Pennsylvania. The very first present I received was from my brother-in-law. It brought me to tears. It was a white sweatshirt with the exact same three angels on it that the nurse had on at the scene of the accident.

I asked Larry what had led him to choose that very sweatshirt for me. He said as he was walking through the store it was as if God was drawing him to that shirt and told him that he should pick that sweatshirt for me. So, he bought it, days before the accident ever happened.

Was it just a random coincidence? No. It was truly our precious God showing me that I was exactly where he wanted me to be, doing

Lessons

exactly what he wanted me to do. I stress to the boys and girls that that very same God that we read all the great stories about in the Bible is just as real today as he was back then. He sees their every move and desires to use them if they will just listen to His voice.

We all should know that we could be chosen to be part of a miracle in God's plan if we just look and listen to His still small voice.

By the way I was so excited by my Christmas gift that I just knew I had to share it with Thelma. I called the Virginia State Police. I explained who I was. then gave them the mile marker of the accident. They told me the name of the hospital that Thelma and her family were taken to.

I made a call and got Thelma on the line. We praised our Lord together for His hand on our lives. She told me that earlier that day her husband had led his brother to the Lord at their Christmas meal. Then, as they were traveling down the highway, it was as if her husband was in a trance of some sort. He was drifting into the middle of the road. She grabbed the steering wheel to keep them from hitting the median and caused the car to flip and slide off the right side of the road.

They had been questioning why God would have allowed such an accident to occur after such a blessing. We realized that God just wasn't done blessing them yet. We realized that the blessing would be shared in Bible classes for many years to come. We just were able to be part of the story.

By the way, Thelma, her husband, and her grandson were going to be just fine. We learned that God's plan all along was to be lifted up and glorified by His presence and His presents. We rejoiced for the longest time on the phone.

God's plan was also that adults and children for the next 30 years or more would marvel over His wonderful works. His path for our lives is such a beautiful story. May we never stop singing His praises.

New Creature

The following wonderful, illustration of having our sins totally removed when we accept Christ helps the boys and girls have a visual that they can't forget ...

> II Corinthians 5:17: *Therefore if any man be in Christ, he is a new creature; old things are passed away; behold, all things are become new.*

To teach this lesson it is necessary to have a small empty glass, some water, a small bottle of iodine, a small container of bleach and a lid from an empty container of some kind. Glued to the inside of the lid should be a small wooden cross. It needs to be only 1-2 inches high, glued to the inside of the lid.

Show the empty glass to the students. Take and drink some of the water so that the students can see that is really pure drinking water. Pour a few inches of the water into the small empty glass. At this point you have pure unpolluted water.

Explain to the boys and girls that this is what our heart looks like when we are born, before sin. The boys and girls then mention a sin that they may have committed. After all, Romans 3:23 tells us that all have sinned. Then one drop at a time, we add iodine as each sin is mentioned. The water gets redder and redder with each drop of iodine. Point out that there is no way we would drink from that glass now.

In the same way, God cannot allow us into Heaven with all that sin in our lives. But God has given us a way to have all that sin removed without a trace remaining.

Before the start of class, a bit of bleach has been put into the lid around the cross. The students are not aware of it. At that point the cross is gradually lowered into the glass of red water. It is then moved around slightly in the glass. As the bleach interacts with the iodine water, the water again appears pure. The students are amazed.

Lessons

The visual of total removal of sins is unforgettable. DO NOT THEN DRINK THE WATER.

You may conclude by explaining that this is not magic, but just a visual to help them picture how our sins are removed by trusting in Jesus. When he enters our heart, all sins are instantly removed, past present and future.

Diet

We once studied the lives of Daniel, Shadrach, Meshach and Abednego. Daniel 1:8 explains that they were different because they ate right. They would not defile themselves with the king's meat, nor with the wine which he drank.

> Daniel 1:12: Prove thy servants, I beseech thee, ten days; and let them give us pulse to eat and water to drink.

We gave the challenge to the boys and girls and the adults in the room that we would for ten days not drink any sugar drink (soda, etc.) nor eat any foods with sugar (chocolate, candy, etc.). little did I know that parents were also wanting to try this with their children.

We agreed that at the end of the two-week period we would compare how we felt to how we were now feeling. It was a wonderful experience to realize how much stronger and more clear-headed we felt after eliminating sugar products from our life. It was super-exciting to hear from the parents, as well. God works in mysterious ways.

Coins

One time we thought about Matthew 6:21: "Where your treasure is, there will your heart be also."

After the lesson I gave each student three coins: a quarter, a dime and a nickel. They were instructed to randomly give a coin to someone— just to experience the joy of giving for no reason whatsoever.

They could only give one coin at a time. No one could receive all the coins. A few of the children wanted to give a coin to their listener. Most of the coins went to school or home. Imagine the surprise when a teacher or a bus driver received a coin with just the explanation that it was a gift just because they loved them.

The next week, we studied John 3:16: "For God so loved the world that he gave His one and only begotten Son that whosoever believed in him should not perish but have everlasting life."

God so loved that he gave just as the boys and girls gave.

Serving Others

We learned how great it was to be able to serve others.

> *Matthew 25:35-40: For I was hungry, and ye gave me meat; I was thirsty, and ye gave me drink; I was a stranger, and ye took me in; Naked and ye clothed me; I was sick, and ye visited me; I was in prison, and ye came unto me. Then shall the righteous answer him, saying, Lord, when saw we thee hungry, and fed thee? Or thirsty, and gave thee drink? When saw we thee a stranger and took thee in? or naked, and clothed thee? And the King shall answer and say unto you, Inasmuch, as ye have done it unto one of the least of these my brethren, ye have done it unto me.*

They learned that there are people all around us that we could help. We just needed to look for them. If Jesus were here, we would surely do it for him.

The boys and girls were instructed to ask God to show them where there was a need and then meet it. They met a variety of needs over the next couple of weeks. Some of those needs continued to be met for a long time after — such things as cutting someone's grass.

One boy found an older lady in his neighborhood to whom his mother brought food periodically. The woman was an invalid. She was in a wheelchair in her house and could only go outside whenever someone was kind enough to take her out. This young boy began to stop at her mailbox, which was at the end of her sidewalk alongside of the road, each day on his way home from school.

He would grab her mail and slip it in a slot in her door so she could get it every day. When we heard of her need, we began to transport her for groceries and doctor's appointments, as well.

> Mark 10:45: *For even the Son of man came not to be ministered unto, but to minister, and to give His life ransom for many.*

God is pleased when we serve others.

Paralyzed Man

We also learned of the faithfulness of real friends.

> Luke 5:18, 19: *And, behold, men brought in a bed a man which was taken with a palsy; and they sought means to bring him in, and to lay him before Jesus. And when they could not find by what way they might bring him in because of the multitude, they went upon the housetop, and let him down through the tiling with his couch into the midst before Jesus.*

Often lessons are best taught by trying to play it out. Through this lesson, the youngsters experienced first-hand how hard it must have been for the four friends to carry their friend on a stretcher for a distance so that they could then imagine how hard it had to be to walk for miles to reach Jesus.

Then the friends had to get the friend on his stretcher up onto the roof, remove tiles and lower him down with ropes into the center of the room. What great friends they had to be. How much easier it would have been to go in the main door, but they couldn't because of the crowd.

At the end of the lesson, each student received a gift – a Triscuit cracker with a cheese man on it. Using squirty cheddar cheese, we put a stick figure man on the cracker to look like a paralyzed man on a cot. Hopefully they will remember this lesson of friendship every time they see squirty cheese.

Lessons like these are often repeated by the students with their parents.

Creation of Man

Teaching the creation of man is always exciting. The importance of the fact that God created everything from nothing is vital.

Sometimes we make clay at home and bring some in so the students can form a man and then try to bring him to life by breathing into them or just saying something to them. It's impossible.

Sometimes they are given a paper bag with a few objects inside like a paper clip, tape, a marble, etc., and then are given the challenge to create. Impossible.

We learn how God created man.

> *Genesis 2:7: And the Lord God formed man of the dust of the ground, and breathed into his nostrils the breath of life; and man became a living soul.*

Getting down on the floor and pretending to form man from the dust of the ground gets their attention. Then getting down even lower to breathe into the pretend nostrils of the pile of dirt is an amazing illustration.

We remind the students that at the very moment that God breathed into Adam, God's very own breath became part of Adam. A part of God was breathed into us, and we became a living soul because we are so precious to our God.

God will never die. We too will never die. We will live somewhere forever. We will not live here but we will live somewhere else. When we have our sins removed and trust in Jesus, a part of God (the Holy Spirit) lives in us again. He left when we first sinned. But he returns to live inside of us when we believe in Jesus.

The lonely, sad, empty part inside us is never fully happy until Jesus comes in to live in us and fill up that space. Sins move out. Forgiveness moves in.

Creation

One lesson on creation focuses on walking through the six days God took to create. What a joy it is to walk the students through the creation story in Genesis 1 with God.

Genesis 1:3	and God said
Genesis 1:4	it was good
Genesis 1:6	and God said
Genesis 1:9	and God said
Genesis 1:10	it was good
Genesis 1:12	and God said
Genesis 1: 14	and God said
Genesis 1:18	it was good
Genesis 1:20	and God said
Genesis 1:21	it was good
Genesis 1:24	and God said
Genesis 1:25	it was good
Genesis 1:26	and God said
Genesis 1:31	it was very good

On each day, God created. At the end of each day, almost, God said it was good. But on day 6 God created animals and then man. At the end of Day 6, God said it was very good. Then he rested.

Sin

The students learned that when God created man, he warned him that all in the garden was his to eat and enjoy. But God said there were two trees that were not to be eaten – the tree of life and the tree of

The Jesus Lady

the knowledge of good and evil. God said that if he ate from the tree of knowledge of good and evil, he would die.

This was told to Adam before Eve was created. I'm sure Adam must have told Eve when she arrived on the scene. This was really important. Then along came Eve.

> Genesis 2:21,22: And the Lord God caused a deep sleep to fall on Adam, and he slept; and he took one of his ribs, and closed up the flesh instead thereof. And the rib, which the Lord God had taken from him, made he a woman, and brought her unto the man.

We next find Eve alone in the garden with a snake named Satan. Now Satan either had wings or legs at the time, because he was later punished by being told he would have to crawl on his belly and eat dust all the days of his life.

> Genesis 3:13: And the LORD God said unto the woman, What is this that thou hast done? And the woman said, The serpent beguiled me, and I did eat.

Bringing in a large stuffed snake always catches the attention of the students. The snake tempted Eve to eat from the forbidden fruit and she did. Eve believed Satan when he said that God just didn't want them to be as smart as he was. He said that if they ate from that tree, they would be as gods. He is such a liar, from the beginning of time.

The fruit, after all was pretty to look at. So, she ate and then gave some to Adam and he ate too. That was a big mistake.

Before the boys and girls get too angry at Adam and Eve for their bad choice, I illustrate our own personal struggle. Just pretend you just came in the door after school. You're really hungry. The kitchen smells absolutely wonderful. It smells like chocolate chip cookies. It is. Mom just made a bunch. They are cooling all over the counter. They are even still warm. It can't get any better than that.

Mom says, "I have to run upstairs to check on your baby brother for a few minutes. I'll be right back. We'll be eating supper soon. Leave the cookies alone."

Lessons

What?! Maybe if I just eat the smallest cookie and just move the others around a bit, she won't even notice. Would that be so bad? Do you feel the temptation? That's what Eve felt when she looked at the pretty fruit that was so pleasant to the eyes.

> Genesis 3:6: *The woman saw that the tree was good for food, and that it was pleasant to the eyes, and a tree to be desired to make one wise, she took of the fruit thereof, and did eat, and gave also unto her husband with her; and he did eat.*

We can understand how hard it is to turn and walk away. Sin has a punishment.

Sacrifice

When Adam and Eve sinned, there had to be a punishment. The first thing that Adam and Eve realized was that they were naked. Babies are fine being naked because they are innocent. They have never sinned. Since we have all sinned, we are not comfortable to be naked around everyone. Right?!

God still loved Adam and Eve after they sinned. He decided to make them clothes to wear so they could hide their nakedness. To do that, an innocent animal had to die. God made clothes for them.

> Genesis 3:21: *Unto Adam and also to his wife did the Lord God make coats of skins and clothed them.*

The poor animal didn't deserve to die. He had done nothing wrong. Because we sin, God sacrificed His own son, Jesus, so that if we believe in him, His death covers our sin. As the animal's blood was poured out in his killing, so was our sweet Jesus' blood.

> John 15:13: *Greater love hath no man than this, that a man lay down his life for his friends.*

Fishers of Men

We teach how God desires for us to tell others about Jesus.

Matthew 4:17: And he saith unto them, "Follow me, and I will make you fishers of men."

Luke 5:6: And when they had let down the net, they enclosed a great multitude of fish; and their net broke.

They had to call their friends from another boat to help them.

Luke 5:10: And Jesus said unto Simon, "Fear not; from henceforth thou shalt catch men."

There were so many fish in the nets that they could hardly pull them all in, yet they left them all on the shore and followed Jesus. Following Jesus is the best thing we can do.

I've brought in one of Paul's large fishing nets while we reenacted this story of the fishermen in two boats. Some of the students had to throw this big net out of their pretend boat into the center of the room. Others were called to help them drag the full net in to the shore, then they were told to leave all the fish behind and follow Jesus.

That would have been worth a lot of money. Money wasn't nearly as valuable as Jesus. They didn't even know where they were going, just that they were going. They went.

Joseph

When the story of Joseph was taught, it was amazing how easily the boys and girls related to blended families. So many of them had half brothers and sisters and wrestled with feelings that they weren't loved as much as the others. Some children had a parent who was gone, and now they had a completely new family and new children.

Lessons

They easily understood the jealousy between Joseph's brothers.

There was quite a big discussion and hurts were shared with one another. Our hearts were breaking just hearing their stories. They understood how angry and jealous the other brothers were when Jacob gave Joseph his coat of many colors.

> Genesis 37:3, 4: Now Israel loved Joseph more than all his children, because he was the son of his old age: and he made him a coat of many colors. And when his brethren saw that their father loved him more than all his brethren, they hated him, and could not speak peaceably unto him.

They surely understood how the brothers sold him into slavery.

> Genesis 37:28: Then there passed by Midianites merchantmen; and they drew and lifted up Joseph out of the pit, and sold Joseph to the Ishmaelites f or twenty pieces of silver.

But the joy of hearing the end of the story was great as they saw that God had a plan larger than their imaginations when Joseph saw his brothers again many years later.

> Genesis 50:20: But as for you, ye thought evil against me; but God meant it unto good, to bring to pass, as it is this day, to save much people alive.

Free Gift

Most children know that at Christmas-time they get gifts. Early in our salvation unit, I bring in a pretty wrapped gift, bow and all. I ask the students what they have to do to get a gift. Is it something you work for? No! It is absolutely free, or else it is not a gift at all. It is something earned.

> Romans 6:23: For the wages of sin is death; but the gift of God is eternal life through Jesus Christ our Lord.

They learn that when they cut someone's grass and hold out their hand to be paid, what they receive is their wage. They've earned it for doing a job. But a gift is not earned but is free. What must they do to receive this gift? I hold the gift out to a student. They must receive it. If they don't reach out and take it, it is still a gift. It just isn't their gift. I will just keep it until they are ready to reach out and receive it.

God holds the gift of eternal life for each one of them until they are ready to accept it. Some people never accept God's free gift of life forever in Heaven. They one day die and then it is too late to take the gift. That's so very sad.

All Have Sinned

It is so important that the boys and girls understand that everyone has sinned. That means their mom, their dad, their grandparents, all the adults in the room and them too.

> *Romans 3:23: For all have sinned and fall short of the glory of God.*

Not only did Adam and Eve sin but we do, too. When they sinned, the punishment of death passed on to all of us because we all sin.

> *Romans 5:19: For as by one man's disobedience many were made sinners, so by the obedience of one shall many be made righteous.*
> *Romans 5:8: But God commends his love toward us, in that, while we were yet sinners, Christ died for us.*

Long before we were born, God saw us. He died for us, knowing we were going to sin, so, he sent Jesus to die for us 2,000 years ago. Believing in Jesus can take away ALL our sins even those we may do later.

The Bible says when we pray, we are placed in God's right hand. His left hand covers over and holds us fast. We are safe with Him and Satan can NEVER pull us back. That's great news.

If we sin again, we just need to tell God we are sorry and ask him to

Lessons

help us to do better next time. He will never let go of us. When we disobey our mom and dad, are we still their child? Yes. They stay our parents even though we may disappoint them. God stays our Father even when we disappoint Him.

Trinity

Another interesting lesson is explaining the Trinity. How can they understand that God the father, Jesus the son and the Holy Spirit are one and the same?

> John 1:1: In the beginning was the Word, and the Word was with God, and the Word was God. The same was with God in the beginning.

> John 1:2: The same was in the beginning with God.

> John 1:14: And the Word was made flesh, and dwelt among us, (and we beheld his glory, the glory as of the only begotten of the Father,) full of grace and truth.

> Genesis 1:1-2: In the beginning God created the heaven and the earth. And the earth was without form, and void; darkness was upon the face of the deep. And the Spirit of God moved upon the face of the waters.

Water can be used as an example. Water can be a vapor such as steam, yet still it is water. Water can be a liquid as water and still be water. Water can be frozen as in ice. Still it's water.

Another example is an egg. The outside of the egg is the shell — still egg. The yolk of the egg is still egg. The white of the egg is still egg.

The Trinity consists of God in Heaven, unseen.

The Trinity is also Jesus, on Earth in a physical body. The Trinity is also the Holy Spirit which lives inside each believer from the moment he or she accepts Christ. All are part of the Trinity and are equally important. All are one.

The Rapture

Matthew 24:40: Then shall two be in the field; the one shall be taken, and the other left.

Matthew 24:44: Therefore be ye also ready; for in such an hour as ye think not the Son of man cometh.

Many years ago, a guest teacher named Ruth had a wonderful lesson to show the boys and girls how one day Jesus would call His believers on the Earth to join him in the air. Not everyone would get to go to Him.

Unbelievers would be left behind here. She cut out pictures of people, similar to old-time paper dolls. Each was glued to a cardboard backing. One was to look like Jesus. Others were adults and children.

The figure of Jesus had magnets glued to the cardboard on the back of each hand (where the children couldn't see them). Some of the other cutouts had paper clips glued in the back of their hands. Others did not.

When Jesus came near, the hands of the figures with paper clips would be drawn to the hands of Jesus. The others did not. They stayed laying down. Only children who had asked Jesus into their heart were able to go with Jesus to Heaven. This was a super-intense visual.

Sword Drills

Our fifth-grade teacher in Wellsville challenges her boys and girls each week to a sword drill to help them get familiar with where the books of the Bible are and how to find scripture by chapter and verse.

She teaches them that first, they must find the book of the Bible. Then the chapter is the first number following the book. It is also found at the top of each page of the book. Following the colon is the verse number.

She has the students hold their Bible in the air with their finger in the Table of Contents, then she says, for example, "John 3:16."

The students repeat John 3:16. Rose gives the command to "GO!" The boys and girls race to be the first to find the verse. Whenever they find the verse, they jump to their feet. Then the rest of the class stands as they, too, find the verse until every student was standing. Often students that are already standing assist the other students so they can find it, too. This helps the boys and girls learn to use their table of contents and find verses for themselves.

Also, in Wellsville Bible Released Time, all of the third-, fourth- and fifth-graders were encouraged to learn a song that puts all of the books of the Bible to a tune. This song was part of our Song Time each week.

By the end of the year most students, as well as staff, learned the books of the Bible. This was a great teaching tool for me to learn where to find things in the Bible as well. Thank you, Rose.

Students Teaching

One year, a student said that she would really love to see what it would be like to be a teacher. She said she always wanted to give it a try. The thought came to me to ask if she wanted to go up to the blackboard and teach the other students about Jesus. She certainly did.

We only had less than a month of classes left for the school year. Other boys and girls said they'd like to teach, too. We saw so many crosses drawn on the blackboard as well as invitations to accept Christ.

Our student teachers were inviting their classmates to accept Jesus and led them in prayer. It was a most memorable time.

Assembly Conflict

Sometimes it seems like life throws us a curve when really it is a direct hit for the Lord and His plan. We end up receiving the biggest gift.

One day, we saw our students arrive for class in tears. It seems they were pulled out of a school assembly where a local TV weatherman was speaking. The students asked to leave were not only loving the assembly, but they also were totally embarrassed by being removed.

We try to watch the elementary school's activities schedule closely and cancel our classes any time there is something planned at the school. Since parents sign up their children to be in Released Time for this specific hour each week, we are responsible for them for that time.

They are permitted to stay at the school with a note from the parent for special events. Students, however, are not permitted to choose to stay at school whenever they desire.

As a result, these students were forced to leave to go the Released Time. Each of them had their name called and were made to rise and walk out in front of their classmates. The assembly ground to a standstill until they all exited.

The staff all joined in prayer and asked God to help us find an answer to this problem that would glorify him. He most surely led us to the correct path to take. I called the TV station and explained the situation to them.

The next thing I knew I got a phone call from Chuck Rhodes, the weatherman himself. When he heard how upset the students were, he decided to personally make it up to them. A few weeks later he (in the flesh) attended our Bible Released Time class.

The brokenhearted boys and girls had the star of the assembly sitting right with them. He sang songs with them and talked to them about the importance of walking right and making good choices.

God had an even better plan all along. God gave them an even bigger

Lessons

treat than what they had missed. The weatherman even got to hear a gospel message. That must have been part of God's plan as well.

The students learned to trust the Lord even more as a result of what started out as a disappointment.

Covid 19

Covid 19 really threw the Bible Released Time program into some new uncharted territory. It was no longer possible to have our group together. School wasn't even in session the usual way. But the program continued.

Now instead of many people meeting at the church, only two showed up – the fifth-grade teacher and a sweet listener who was also our piano teacher/song leader. The two of them recorded an hour of singing, announcements and teaching for the absent class. These recordings were then emailed to the student's home.

It was then not only watched by the child but by parents, as well. They could watch at the parents' convenience. Listeners would call the homes once a week to listen to verses that the child had memorized. The verses had to be recited in the presence of a parent. This meant that the verse was also running through the minds of parents.

A real bond was being formed between some parents and the child's listener. One listener, Wally, was asked to keep calling the home every Saturday evening to talk to his student. He was asked to continue calling all summer long on Saturday evening. The bond with the parents ended up being much deeper as a result.

Many of the listeners have kept in contact with their boys and girls long into their adulthood through mail and phone calls.

Many of our students are second-generation children. We either taught their parents first or their parents were volunteers at some time. Now their children are being taught in Bible Released Time. What a joy!

Homeschool

The Bible Released Time program is not only available to public school students. It is also available to those students that are being home schooled. We often have a few home-schooled students that are dropped off for classes and picked up an hour later.

Sometimes the parents chose to stay and help or observe. Sometimes they go home.

One year, a mom who home-schooled her children came in to check us out. After the first week, she enrolled her daughter as a student and an older daughter as a helper. As they grew up, as teenagers, they became part of our program. One played the piano. They both listened to verses.

Cancer

All of life can be turned into teachable moments. One song leader and listener/teacher were diagnosed with cancer. The staff and children all knew her and loved her. She was open about her cancer from the get-go.

The students watched God's hand on her life as she was facing chemotherapy and would be losing her hair. Instead of letting them be worried about her, she took a different approach. She and another friend/listener, Caroline, went and got their heads shaved together. When they came into class with their bald heads, Judy explained why they had done it. The boys and girls as well as all staff were touched with the compassion that Caroline for Judy, evidenced by getting her head shaved even though her hair was fine. Her heart was finer.

As a group, we bought and made hats for the two of them. The boys and girls walked that walk with her. Near the end of Judy's ability to teach, she decided to hang her many hats on the end of the sanctuary pews. Then she had the boys and girls vote on their favorite hats. They had a great time doing this.

Judy continued to teach the students music. I remember before

Christmas, Judy taught them the song "Ring those Bells." She said that it was her favorite song. Not long after that, God called Judy home. The most beautiful music at her funeral was when the students sang her favorite song. Hearts were touched as they heard:

> Come on ring those bells
> Everybody say:
> Jesus, we remember this
> Your birthday.

Judy's life was a forever lesson in trusting the Lord, God whatever His plan. They learned through her teachings that God was her constant companion even in what the world would call her darkest days. They witnessed first-hand the peace of God and how they could trust whatever he chose for them in their life.

Psalms 119

At the beginning of each school year, we teach what we call the introductory lessons. These verses are all taken from Psalms 119 and show the boys and girls how important God's Word is.

Psalms 119:11: Thy word have I hid in my heart, that I might not sin against thee.

Psalms 119:89: Forever, O Lord, thy word is settled in Heaven.

Psalms 119:105: Thy word is a lamp unto feet and a light unto my path.

When we memorize God's word, we are hiding it deep in our heart so that we always remember it even if someone would steal our Bible. Having scripture memorized, we have help to keep us from falling into sin.

To help them remember the scripture reference, I point out that when we are in big trouble, we learn to call 911. When we need God's help to keep us out of trouble, we find the answer in 119:11. That's 911 coming and going. That's why we learn scripture to keep us from an emergency later.

We learn that God's word is forever settled. It never changes even though it is 2,000 years old. The same rules apply today for a happy life. Don't steal. Don't lie. Obey your father and mother. Love one another. And on and on.

God doesn't have to write anything new in the Bible. It is enough. If our family has a car and it breaks down, what book do we need to pick up to see how to fix it? A math book? A cookbook? NO! You would need a car manual.

If we want to know what God calls sin so we don't do it, what book do we need to pick up to see how to fix it? A math book? A cookbook? NO! The Bible.

We should hide verses in our heart so we know how to live to please God. Then we learn how learning scripture lights our path so we don't go doing bad things and getting punished.

We remember where this is found in chapter 119 by picturing the 105. Picture the 0 in the middle as our light (flashlight) to help us see our way.

Forgiveness

While preparing to teach about loving one another, God led me to ask forgiveness of someone before I could, in all conscience, teach the lesson to the students.

> John 15:12: This is my commandment, that ye love one another, as I have loved you.

God quickly revealed a sin to me. It was important that I ask a co-worker for forgiveness first. This wasn't going to be easy. You see she wasn't even aware of my sin. Over the years a lesson just falls flat when the teacher needs to first get herself right with the Lord. At this moment that's where I found myself.

One day while I was working part-time in the school district office, I overheard some other girls discussing another worker. They were sharing how unkind she was. Then they turned to me and said that

I wouldn't know about that because I just worked part time. Before I knew it, I was joining in to say, "Oh yes I do know."

Then I proceeded to fill them in on an instance that she was unkind to me. She had jumped all over me one Saturday when I felt led to call her at home to ask her a work-related question. She said she didn't work from at home over the weekend. I would need to ask her when she came in on Monday. Then she hung up. How rude.

Not only did she seem rude. I was even ruder because I just became part of a group of people talking behind someone's back. I was no better.

God impressed on me that I needed to ask her forgiveness for my actions. I didn't call her at home to ask her. The next day I pulled her aside and explained what I had done. I asked her to forgive me because that was wrong. She said that was OK because everyone talks bad about her.

That didn't make what I did any less wrong. The blessing of the Lord wouldn't have been possible with my troubled conscience. Eventually she forgave me and the boys and girls learned a valuable lesson on love and forgiveness as I shared my story.

Some students even went across the room to another student to seek forgiveness. Often, our own life needs to be a lesson in itself. After all, we are not perfect. Why pretend to be?

Lion's Den

Role-playing is so memorable as a teaching tool. Rose, our fifth-grade teacher once taught a lesson about Daniel in the lions' den from the perspective of the lion. As her students were sitting in the seats in the sanctuary, she (in a full-body lion's costume) crawled up the aisle from the back of the church.

The students were totally unaware of what was going on as they kept looking forward wondering where their teacher was. As you can imagine, she scared a number of her boys and girls as she quietly crawled next to their legs or brushed against some of them.

She went to the front of the class and told the whole story of Daniel being thrown into the lions' den from the perspective of one of the lions. It was wonderfully acted out. I'm sure this class is still remembered vividly by both the students and the adults in the room.

Donkey

One teacher, Leesa, made her Palm Sunday lesson truly memorable to the boys and girls. Instead of just telling the story of Jesus riding into Jerusalem on the back of a donkey amid palm branches, she brought in a real live donkey. She lived on a small farm and was able to bring in a beautiful little donkey.

She showed the students how the donkey even had a cross on its back. This was a sign that God put on the donkey as proof of this most wonderful story.

She even brought in a camera and took pictures of each boy and girl with the donkey that she later gave them to take home. What a brilliant story that they will never forget.

12 Disciples

One lesson that was taught to fourth- and fifth-graders had to do with the 12 disciples of Jesus. The teacher wanted to let the children know that the disciples were important to Jesus but so were they. The original song went like this:

There were 12 disciples Jesus called to help him:

Simon Peter, Andrew, James, his brother John;

Phillip, Thomas, Mathew,

James the son of Alpheus, Thaddeus,

Simon, Judas and Bartholomew.

        (chorus)

He has called us, too. He has called us, too.

We are his disciples. I am one. Are you?

He has called us too. He has called us, too.

We are his disciples. We his work must do.

In the 2021-2022 year, there 16 students in her fourth- and fifth-grade class. Not to be out done, she created a song that went like this:

There were 16 disciples Jesus calls to help him.

Ella, Rylie, Carrington, Mason, Crue and Layne

Jonah, Brianna, Jaici, Braydon, Willow, Jaden,

Nick, Riley, Julian, and Trinity!

(chorus)

He has called us too. He has called us, too.

We are his disciples. I am one. Are you?

He has called us too. He has called us, too.

We are his disciples. We his work must do!

The students absolutely loved it. They each realized that they, too, had a job to do for the Lord as his disciple. What a creative way to present a lesson.

Repeat

On January 26, 2018, a text was sent out by the Bible Released Time coordinator of the Wellsville program to the staff that made me chuckle. You may enjoy it just as much. Here it is:

Just need to share with you all my "wrap up" of yesterday. I keep thinking about it this morning and chuckling as to the faith of children!! Visualize Jan seated on the bottom step of the altar area surrounded by children. They were all eagerly listening (well perhaps one or two were wriggling). She is explaining Jesus speaking to and teaching Nicodemus. At the conclusion, Carter raised his hand and said, "Well, I bet he needed to hear that more than once!" Don't we all?

Christmas

The boys and girls enjoy when we put on a Christmas play and they get to act out the parts. We plan to perform on an evening so their parents can attend. They perform in full dress outfits—crowns, wings, manger and all.

One wonderful play, we had three shepherds just off the altar area, near the kneelers, and that's where they were told to stay after they followed the star up the aisle.

Don't you know—one of the shepherds didn't just keep low so the audience could see, but laid down instead, and fell fast asleep while the play went on. Talk about a memorable moment!

One year, we did a dress up Christmas play in which they were a part but it was during the day during our usual time for having the children. Much to their absolute surprise in walked one of the wise men in full dress that they recognized. It was the principal of their school who was a fine Christian man who wanted to surprise them and be in the play too. They were in their glory.

Surprises are always possible when God is in charge.

Easter

There are so many ways to present the Easter lesson – from reading the Easter story from a book to reading from the Bible. Once, I bought a large picture in a frame from a yard sale—featuring three combined scenes: Golgotha, Jerusalem and the empty tomb.

I brought it to class and had a piece of paper taped to cover each of the three scenes. As I talked about the scene of Jerusalem, I uncovered that part of the picture. Then, I talked about the death of Christ and uncovered the scene of Golgotha. Finally, they heard about the joyous rising of our Lord from the grave. When I uncovered the empty tomb, it was a great moment.

Each year, that picture accompanied me to class.

Lessons

Jericho

Teaching the story of Joshua and the walls of Jericho can be so exciting when reenacted by the boys and girls.

Reading the story from Joshua 6 is a great place to start. We, then, have the boys and girls walk around the sanctuary once a day quietly. On Day Seven, we have them walk around seven times, blow a whistle and imagine the walls coming down.

Fortunately, New Year's Eve-style blow-out whistles can be found almost year-round at the dollar store in the party supply section.

Thirst

The boys and girls at Bible Released Time know that they are not permitted to drink water or chew gum in class. The same rules that they must obey in school pertain to class here, as well.

> Psalms 42:2: My soul thirsts for God, for the living God.

It is my great honor to bring a nice cold bottle of water to my classroom when it is time to teach this lesson. As the students sit obediently before me, I raise the bottle of water to my mouth and take a really big drink. They are completely amazed.

So, I ask them how they feel about that. They fully understand the meaning of thirsting after something. I then proceed to teach the lesson. In the same way, my soul thirsts for God. The more I spend time in my Bible, the more time I want to spend. I thirst more and more.

God So Loved

When teaching John 3:16, here's a way to really help the boys and girls relate to the verse.

John 3:16: For God so loved the world that he gave his only begotten son, that whosoever believeth in him, should not perish, but have everlasting life.

Sometimes the boys and girls relate to that verse so much more when you insert their own name in the verse. For example: "For God so loved Mike that he gave His only begotten son, that if Mike believes in him, Mike should not perish but have everlasting life."

Ten Commandments

Sometimes, it is really hard for the boys and girls to learn the Ten Commandments. A song has helped us at Bible Released Time to teach the Ten Commandments much easier. It goes like this:

No other gods. No idols
Don't misuse God's name
Keep the Sabbath holy
That's God's special day. Hey!
Honor your father and your mother
Don't murder, lust or steal
No false tales. Don't envy
This is God's great deal. Hey!

The "Hey" at the end is yelled as a cheer. This has helped every child and adult learn their Ten Commandments.

Psalms 23

In closing, I need to share something that really helps the boys and girls to learn the last verse of the 23rd Psalm.

I hang name signs on three children. They read: Shirley, Goodness, and Mercy.

I pretend they are little sheep and they follow me all around. In other words, Shirley, Goodness and Mercy follow me all the days of my life. How corny is that?

There is nothing too corny to use to teach a child. They love it all.

Miracles

Nancy

Right after the night Christ changed my life, a young girl came to my mind. She was the daughter of the man from whom my late husband and I rented.

Let me back up...My young life was full of trouble. At age 18, I left home, just two weeks after graduation. When I was 24, I was blessed with my first son, Tom. His dad and I were married and happy, but one day when Tom was just 6 months old, his dad died.

I was angry with God. My Catholic roots told me that there was a God who could have chosen to let him stay here but chose to take him. I lived with that anger for eight years and made many bad choices during that time.

After my husband died, I was saved. Nancy, the landlord's daughter, gave me a phone call. She knew I was struggling and handling the loss poorly. She was just a teenager who loved the Lord, her God. She called to tell me there was someone who truly loved me. His name was Jesus Christ.

I was definitely full of anger over what I felt God allowed to happen, leaving me alone with a 6-month-old son. I told her I couldn't talk and hung up.

Eight years later, loving the same Lord but with a different heart, I called my landlord from way back then. After sharing my new belief in Jesus Christ, I asked for Nancy's phone number. She was married and living far away from home. Imagine her surprise and joy when I thanked her for her faithful prayers for me. God had finally answered those prayers. She and I rejoiced together.

Misdirected

Those eight years were really held strongly by Satan. I made so many bad choices. Because I was so full of anger toward God, I put up many walls in my life.

The Jesus Lady

I thought that since my son didn't have a dad, I should marry the first person who asked me to marry him. I became a regular at a neighborhood bar. There, I met the bartender. Later, I ended up marrying him and becoming a captive in a very abusive marriage. A pastor took us in until I could move out on my own.

I went from there to say, "OK. I will remain single forever and never fall in love again. That way I couldn't be hurt, and God could never take away someone I loved again."

When Tom was 3 years old, I met a married man who wanted to spend time with me. He was married. That felt safe to me. We could never love each other because he belonged to someone else. In my confusion, I felt safe. With blinders on, I never considered his wife.

On accepting Christ, God firmly put his wife on my mind. I had surely been responsible for their marriage falling apart. I gave her a call at her place of employment and asked her to meet me for lunch.

She said she had no car, so my only way to get this accomplished was to pick her up in my own car. She was saved as a little girl, so she must have known God had a plan beyond her wildest expectations.

Linda allowed me to pick her up. We went to McDonald's. Just call me a big spender. Amid tears, I apologized to her and asked her to forgive me. I shared how the Lord had just saved me and I would do all I could to help her get her marriage back with Paul.

She forgave me but now had someone else in her life. She very wisely pointed out that by that time, Paul and I had a daughter, and we should stay together. As a Catholic girl who only knew that marriages are for life, I didn't know what to do if he couldn't go back.

She was kind enough to understand why I felt safe spending time with a married man. She was my first example of the forgiveness of God and a love and understanding that truly covers our sin.

As the years went on, she and I became very close. We went to the same church, her church from the time she was little. She and her husband as well, as Paul and I, all went there together.

Miracles

She headed up the Junior Church. Often, we would meet in her classroom before the boys and girls arrived and pray together for our children and grandchildren. I loved and respected her so much.

Later in life, she got cancer. We prayed for God's healing. God chose to heal her in Heaven. A few weeks before her death, we attended a grandson's wedding. At the reception, was a joyful little group of four. Linda, Ron, Paul and I were at the end of one of the tables, just laughing and enjoying each other.

One of my most treasured blessings was Paul and I sitting at the foot of her hospital bed in her last days. God showed me once again how he can bring beauty from ashes. No sin is too great to be forgiven.

Paul

At the time I was saved, I had my son, Tom, who was 8 years old and my 2-year-old daughter, Suzie. Paul was the father of Suzie. Paul and I were living together at the time but not married. Right away, I was convicted of the sin in my life. He was visiting with his children when I prayed at the side of my bed. He was shocked and taken aback when he returned and I told him he would have to move out.

Of course, he couldn't begin to understand where that was coming from. To him, it seemed that we were just a happy little family. Before I was saved, I would have agreed.

God knew that what I needed more than anything was to spend undistracted time with my Lord alone. Sin had no place in my life anymore. For the next two and a half years, I hungered and thirsted for more and more of Jesus.

My son, Tom, began attending a small Christian school. We were there every time the church doors opened. My Bible went everywhere I went. I listened to Christian tapes and Christian radio non-stop. This sponge was soaking up all it could get. I was putty in the hands of the Lord.

My poor Paul learned to wait on the Lord right out of the gate – when I made him move out from our little home. He was lost. He stayed with a brother for a while, then he got a small place of his own. From time to time, he would come around to take me to dinner or pick up the kids for a while, but I only wanted my time with Jesus.

Paul was my closest friend, but Jesus was No. 1. From time to time, Paul would ask me to marry him. My answer was always, "No." I knew we couldn't be unequally yoked. I had learned that much. He needed to be saved, so we would be on the same page.

Then one night, Paul visited and asked if I'd give Pastor Norris a call because Paul wanted to pray to be saved. The pastor came and prayed with him to accept Christ. As soon as the pastor went out the door, Paul asked me to marry him. I said, "No," once again. I felt that he just prayed so that I would marry him.

I questioned how genuine the prayer was. I wanted him to love Jesus as much as I did. What did I expect? The man had just been saved.

He began to attend the same church we were going to. As he grew and time went on, he even met a sweet girl who he led to the Lord. She attended church with him each Sunday. God had replaced my love for Paul with a strong friendship. There was no jealousy between us.

Then one day, I was reading, studying my Bible and listening to teaching tapes, in this instance a tape series by John McArthur about divorce and remarriage. He stressed how on accepting Christ we become a new creation. Old things are passed away and all things become new. We are then a new creature in Christ.

At the time of our salvation, if we are married, we should remain married. If we are divorced, we should just remain single until God changes our path. He used the illustration of holding out a raw egg and dropping it on the ground. It shatters beyond repair. You can't put the pieces back together again. You cannot go back and put a marriage back together again. I was wrong when I tried to help Linda years ago.

I wasn't sure what the Lord was telling me, so I told him I would just be still until he revealed to me whether I should ever think of marriage again or not. I only wanted what he wanted for me. I was 100% content with where I was.

Miracles

His answer totally caught me off guard. God had me fall deeply and purely in love with Paul. Needless to say, my prayer time became times of intense fellowship with my Lord. Like, "Why now? Why not one of the many times he asked me to marry him when he was alone? Someone else will be hurt now just like Linda was. God your timing stinks."

I'm sure God was saying, "Be still, my child. Trust me."

A few days later, I was invited to Paul's place for a birthday party for his son David. David and Tom are only six weeks apart in age and were close. I packed up the kids and headed out. When I got there, Paul was sitting on a chair and his girlfriend, Laurie, was standing behind him with her hands gently on his shoulders. Instantly I felt crushed. I went into the bathroom and cried. When I came out, I said I wasn't feeling well and would need to go home – and I left.

Later that week, my car decided to break down. I know now it was the plan of God. Paul was called to come look at it since he was, after all a car mechanic. As he worked on the car in my driveway, I stood inside crying.

When he was finished, he came in. He entered and knew right away that I had been crying. He asked what was wrong. I sat him down and went through the whole egg story. I asked if he'd just consider taking me out now and then while I sort out these feelings.

He replied, "I'll consider taking you out now and then if you consider marrying me. You're all I ever wanted. I just didn't think you'd ever say, "Yes." Obviously, I didn't, either.

Only God saw this day coming. God also knew it would take over two years for the timing to be right. We were married four months later. The timing was perfect.

Annette

When I had only been attending our little church for a short time, I met my sweet neighbor, Annette. She and her husband were raising her younger brother and sister since her parents were no longer around.

They lived just up the street. Tom and her brother, Louie, were the same age. One Sunday, Tom invited Louie and his sister to our church. They not only visited but accepted Christ, as well. They were so happy to show us the Bibles they received on this great day.

After we got home, they walked up the street to their home. Before too much time had gone by, they returned to our door. They each held their new Bible in their hand. Their sister informed them that they were no longer allowed to attend church with us. I learned that their sister was Catholic and these Bibles were not allowed in their home. Since I, too, had been Catholic, I asked if they would tell their sister that I'd love to meet her. They went back home.

In just a short while, this kind sister was at my door. I sat her at my kitchen table. I pointed out that I knew just what she was tormented by since I had been raised the same way. A mortal sin (the worst kind) was committed when you attended any church that was not Catholic. Worse yet, these kids brought home a Bible (also not Catholic).

I tried to help her understand my joy in going to church. The Catholic church teaches that not to go to church is a sin. I just loved to spend time with Jesus, I told her, I no longer prayed to Mary and the saints but went straight to Jesus.

I invited her to come with us just once, and she came the following Sunday. Then, much to my surprise, she went forward to give her heart to the Lord. I broke down in tears. The pastor looked at me and asked – if I could stop crying long enough – would I please take Annette back to pray with her.

We went to the back and I thanked God for her decision. I asked God to forgive her sins and take her to Heaven when she died. I probably left out things, but God accepted her, and Annette became my best friend. Afterward, she, her brother and her sister went to church with us every time we went. She even became part of the choir.

Evelyn

I began to practice Mark 16:15: Preach the Gospel to all men. When my son, Tom, was a baby, it became necessary for me to go to work since his dad was no longer alive to take care of us. A sweet older woman, who lived on the block behind our place, became his babysitter.

Tom was 8 when I was saved. It was about two years later that God brought Evelyn to my mind. I mean he REALLY brought her to my mind. For about two days, I couldn't stop of thinking of her. Finally, I decided God must want me to go visit her.

It had been nearly ten years since I had seen her. I got in my car and drove about half an hour to the block where she lived. There was no house there anymore. It was just a vacant lot. I questioned what God expected me to do now.

I remembered that Evelyn's daughter used to live on the next block over. I drove to her house and went up her steps. At least I hoped they were still her steps.

This woman opened the door and I asked if her mom's name was Evelyn. It was. I asked if Evelyn was still alive since her house was no longer standing. She informed me that Evelyn now lived in a little apartment less than a block away that could only be entered by the alley.

She explained to me how to get to her sidewalk from the alley. I followed her directions, parked my car and walked up the sidewalk. I knocked and waited. I heard steps coming to the door. The next thing I knew, Evelyn opened the door.

She invited me into her kitchen. There on her table was an open Bible. She had been talking to her son who was in prison on death row. While in prison, he had accepted Christ. He was in another state and hadn't seen his mom is a very long time.

His desire was that his mom too would accept Christ. He had told her that she could find Jesus in the Bible. That's what she was attempting to do.

My heart wanted to burst with happiness when I realized that my God had called me to her home to lead her to Him in answer to her son's prayer. God knew that I would respond to his call. If I wouldn't have gone, he would have sent someone else.

With tremendous joy I prayed with Evelyn right there in her kitchen to trust Christ as her personal savior. With a new bounce in my step, I began my drive home.

Here's where the tears flow. About two weeks after my visit with Evelyn, she passed away. God knew the window of opportunity to have her son's prayer be answered was just two weeks. As a result, He put her on my heart and was relentless.

I went to her funeral and was overjoyed to share with the rest of her family the surety that Evelyn was now joyously in Heaven because of her choice two weeks prior. I'm forever honored that God chose me to sit with her at her quiet kitchen table that day. Now whenever God leads me to share Him, I don't hesitate.

Catholic Priest

At some point after becoming a Christian, it dawned on me that I was still on the roll of the Catholic church. There was no way if I died that I wanted a priest to show up for my funeral. All I wanted was my Baptist pastor.

I set out to drive to the Catholic church with the sole intention of getting my name removed from their roll. A priest answered the door and took me down the hall to a little room. I began to explain how I was no longer Catholic and wanted my name removed. He said, "What will your mother and dad have to say about that?" I would so disappoint them, he said.

I shared that my son was now in a Christian school, and we were attending a Baptist church. I said I knew I was no longer Catholic. He wanted to know what I meant by that.

I proceeded to tell him how I had asked Jesus Christ to come into my heart and forgive my sins. This man believed only a priest could forgive sins. I saw him begin to fidget. He began to look at his watch. He announced that he had to cut this visit short because he needed to get ready for a mass or some other such excuse.

We were walking down the hall toward the front door. As he reached for the door, God pressed on my heart that this man was lost in sin and was on his way to Hell, no matter what he believed.

I told him that on this day, I was going to begin to pray for him. He stopped dead in his tracks, his hand still on the doorknob. He turned to me and asked, "Why would you pray for me?"

I said I would pray that he might come to know Christ as his own personal Savior. Then he saw me out the door. A few weeks later his name was in the paper because he was no longer at that church. Could he have found Christ and left? I may never know. But God does.

Bob

Is anything too hard for God? A sweet friend from my Wednesday morning Bible study group shared that her dad was near death in his bed at home. I had met her dad, Bob, while doing my job of census-taking over the years.

Bob was a quiet Quaker man. We would have discussions comparing Christianity to Quaker beliefs. We were always kind to each other but we each held firm to our own beliefs. He wasn't buying this salvation message. We were just friends but that's all.

I asked Bonnie to pray, because right after Bible study, I was going to make a run to his house. The girls prayed and I drove off. His caretaker answered the door when I arrived. He said that Bob had not been alert in quite some time. He would however show me to Bob's room if I desired. I did.

I held Bob's hand as he laid there perfectly still with his eyes closed. As far as I could tell, he was totally unaware of my being in the room. I asked him if he wanted to trust in Jesus as his Savior. He never answered.

Just in case he was at all alert and aware of my presence, I decided to pray out loud, imagining he couldn't respond after me. As I was praying, I noticed a tear in his eye. Then as I said "Amen" and began to rise from my chair, I heard his strong voice say, "I'll see you later, Jan."

He was so loud that the caretaker came running. He was surely saved. I couldn't wait to call Bonnie to share answered prayer.

Earl

As a result of my traveling all over the streets of my town and going to over 8,000 homes, God gave me so many open doors to pray with folks. It was definitely not a job, but my mission field.

In the course of my job, I met a man named Earl. He was sort of a grumpy old man. He had a need that I could meet. His daughter had stopped helping him with his checkbook and he didn't know how to pay his own bills. I began to help him each month with his bills.

He wasn't always the most pleasant person, but he appreciated the help I gave him. Eventually the day came that he felt so depressed that he called me at the Admin Office to tell me he wanted to take his own life.

I left the office and drove to his house. We spent time talking about where he would find himself if he were successful in taking his life. Before I left, he had prayed to accept Christ as his Savior.

I headed back to the office. Work must go on. Later that day a fellow employee led Earl into my office. He wanted to see me. Right behind him walked the superintendent of the school district. Earl turned to the superintendent and said, "It's a beautiful day. Jan just prayed with me to be saved. I'm going to Heaven."

Brian looked right at me and at the smile on Earl's face and said, "Well, have a wonderful day." What else could he say?

Nashville Wheelchair

One time, I begged God to show me his presence as I was about to go through a very painful situation. He showed his face in such a powerful way.

Miracles

My parents had summoned as many of their children down to their home in Nashville to help them make their funeral arrangements. I was dreading this whole ordeal, because there were some very painful family dynamics going on at the time. I needed some time alone with my Lord. He knew what I really needed.

At the entrance to their apartment complex was a nursing home. On the other side of the street from the nursing home was a walking path in a public park. I planned to just walk the path and talk to the Lord.

I walked to the park and sat down at a nearby picnic table. As I began to plead to the Lord to help me get through the day, I looked across the street to the nursing home. I became aware of a man sitting in a wheelchair at the back of the building. He was all alone. I felt God wanted me to go over and maybe cheer him up. I felt the pull of the Holy Spirit and began my walk across the street.

I entered the nursing home and inquired about the man in the wheelchair. The staff informed me that the man had been involved in a traffic accident in which his wife was killed. He had not uttered a word since he arrived in the nursing home.

I asked if they would permit me to go out back to speak to him. They gave their approval. Just then, I saw him start to leave the lot and motor his wheelchair to the park across the street. I took off out the door, calling his name. He seemed to be totally ignoring me. I tried to catch up with him, but he was much faster.

He never even looked my way. I thought that was really rude, but I was sure that the Lord was giving me the push to speak to him. Not only did he go in the direction of the park, but before I could catch up with him, he entered the path that wove around the trees in the park.

I sat at the same picnic table that I had been sitting at not so long ago and I waited. And I waited. Eventually I saw him come down the path in the general direction of where I was sitting. I stood up and called him by name.

He saw me before him and removed the earplugs that he was wearing. Who knew? I guess he really wasn't rude after all! He had no idea I wanted to speak to him.

The Jesus Lady

I got down on his level and talked to him about Jesus. I told him I was aware of the pain in his life and how very special he was to Jesus. He was so special that God chose to send His son to Earth to die in his place.

Right there in the middle of my situation, God allowed this man to accept Jesus Christ as his personal Savior. Then, he smiled and spoke for the first time since the accident, thanking me for taking time to talk to him.

He returned to the nursing home across the street a totally different man than he was such a short time before. I returned to my mother and dad a changed woman. God met with me and refocused my mind. With God all things are possible.

Gas on 74

One day, on my way into town, I saw a young woman walking along the road just crying her eyes out. I stopped to see if I could help in any way. Her car had run out of gas on a side road just a short distance back as she was on her way to get some assistance from a local charity called New Hope Ministries.

She had an appointment but now she was late for it. I sat her in my car and made a call to New Hope. They said that they were sorry but she'd have to reschedule for the next week. It was, after all, a Friday afternoon and they were closing.

She had been hoping to get some food and was desperate. There were more tears. She had no money for food much less gas.

We drove to her apartment for a gas can, and as we rode, I began to tell her how God has a plan that we are often unaware of. It is just His plan. This seemed to be the darkest of situations for her.

As we drove, I introduced her to Jesus. She listened attentively. On our way into town, I pulled my car into the Game Land parking lot and was blessed to lead her to the Lord. What a glorious day!

We went to the local supermarket, and I told her to pick up some groceries to help her get by until Monday. We proceeded to get gas. Our next stop was her car. She and I poured the gas into her car.

We hugged and after I heard her car start up, I went home. What a wonderful day God had planned for her. She just didn't know it.

She never did get my name. It was important that only God get all the glory. I was just His chosen instrument.

Dad

Is there anything too hard for God? Definitely not! My father-in-law was a typical, backwoods, whiskey-drinking man from the hills of West Virginia. He was not a mean man. He drank because of all he had experienced during World War II. So many times, Paul and I tried to share Christ with him but he didn't want to hear it. We were wasting our time. He shut us down every time.

Then, he was diagnosed with pancreatic cancer. He was given a very short time to live. All of the family from Pennsylvania piled into cars and took the long trip to West Virginia to see him one more time. The cars held his kids, grandkids and great-grandkids.

My prayer was that God would let me have some time with him alone. That seemed to be a pretty tall order. He sat in his chair in the living room while everyone stood around in the room and visited with him.

At one point we went to the kitchen for a bite to eat. When food was being devoured by starving travelers, I glanced into the living room. There Dad sat all alone on his chair. This was my sign from God.

I went in and sat on the floor at his feet. I unwrapped and rewrapped his legs with the Ace bandage that he needed because of swelling. All the while, I told him about Jesus. Finally, I asked him if he would like me to pray with him to trust Christ. He did. We held hands and prayed.

With tears rolling down his face, he prayed to give his heart to our Lord. This was the appointed time. We rejoiced all the way back to Pennsylvania to know that we would see him again in Heaven. Praise God. He died shortly after.

Aunt Lu

One year, my mother and dad came up from Tennessee for a family reunion that was planned in Western Pennsylvania. Aunt Lu, my mother's sister, lived in Lancaster. As soon as my mother arrived in town, we all visited Aunt Lu.

Aunt Lu was in a great deal of pain. My mother insisted that she go to the hospital to be checked out. They admitted her that same day. The next day, we left for the family reunion about three hours away.

A phone call came that afternoon for my mother from Uncle Mart, Aunt Lu's husband. Uncle Mart gave her the disturbing news that the doctors had found that Aunt Lu was full of cancer. They just closed her up, determining that they could do nothing for her. She was just going to die.

We left the family reunion right away and headed to her hospital room. The three hours just dragged on and on. While my mother stressed that she didn't believe the hospital would even allow her into intensive care to see her own sister, I used the time in the car to beg God to do the impossible and allow me to have time to pray with her to accept Christ.

My mother made sure I knew that my chances of seeing my Aunt Lu were impossible. I was only the niece. She was a sister. But my God can do the impossible.

When we arrived at the hospital, we were shown the way to the ICU waiting room. There we sat waiting. Finally, my Uncle Mart came in, saying that Aunt Lu was very upset because she thought the hospital had lost her rings.

Mother said perhaps he should check the lost and found. He said to me, "Jan, would you go with me to check the lost and found?" I left with him.

As only God can orchestrate, my uncle walked me right through the intensive care unit. At one point he said, "Your Aunt Lu is right on the other side of this curtain. If you'd like to see her while I go to the lost and found, you can."

Miracles

I almost jumped right through the curtain. He went on his way. There laid my favorite aunt in the world. She was all hooked up to wires and tubes and was intubated, so she was unable to speak at all.

She saw me and reached for me. I told her all about Jesus. I then asked if she wanted us to pray for her to accept Him as her Savior. She nodded. I prayed. She cried.

I promised her that she would be in Heaven when she left this world, and I would be seeing her there. I promised her that I would share with Uncle Mart, at well. She nodded and cried.

Months later, my mother, dad and I were visiting Uncle Mart. As I sat at his feet, he prayed with me to accept Christ, as well. He knows he will be with Aunt Lu forever. Praise our most holy Lord. What a blessing.

Florida

On Christmas Eve 2018, our son, Tom gave us a picture of a home in Florida. He said that he had bought it for us to retire in. We could be "snow birds" and live there all the time, or try it and say we didn't like it. Either way would be OK with him. He just wanted us to know it was his gift to us.

I had the staff of Bible Released Time pray with me as I cried. I hated to leave my students and friends that I had served with for over thirty years. These friendships run deep.

I never thought I would live anywhere other than Pennsylvania, but I didn't want to disappoint him by saying I wasn't going to try. So, in January 2019, I went to Florida to see this home. As soon as I walked in the door, I felt the love of God surround me. I knew I was home. The only heartbreaking thing was giving up my service to Bible Released Time.

I began to pray that God would show me how to fill the void left from the boys and girls at Bible Released Time. He has. Many opportunities to share Christ with others have arisen down here. Sometimes an occasion presents itself at yard sales, for instance.

One time I even got to go to the hospital to share. I had spent the day earlier with my sister in the emergency room. She was having pain and health issues. We were at the hospital all day.

By the way, my sister lives just across the yard from me. That is a blessing in itself. We have not lived in the same state since we were teenagers. Now in our 70s, we are having the time of our lives.

We arrived home around 10 that evening. I had been so concerned about her that I never left her side to get anything to eat. I only allowed myself one drink—a big bottle of Pepsi—all day. When I got home, I heated a bit of leftovers. Then I went to bed.

I woke up again hungry. I thought I'd just get a snack. When I got to the kitchen, I put some cookies and milk on the table. When I went to sit down, I passed out. The chair and I hit the floor. My husband called out from the bedroom to see if I was OK. I bravely said, "Yes ... no."

He came right out and helped me up. Right away, I passed out a second time. The next day, I called my doctor. He wanted me to be admitted overnight for observation.

That night at the hospital, a woman was brought into my hospital room in really bad shape. She was scared. We hit it off right away. We parted the curtain from between us and got to know each other and shared the time together.

We determined to stay in touch when we left the hospital. We talked at length about how Jesus had worked in my life. I realized I may have just one opportunity to share His love with her.

The next day I was sent home. Marcia went home a few days later. She had been sent home to die. We never got to get together again. I pray that God has used something I shared with her to draw her to accept Him as her Savior and Lord.

Paul

The fields are truly white unto harvest. Now instead of children, God has expanded my territory to older people.

One Sunday, I went to the local bank to make a withdrawl from their ATM. After I was finished, I noticed a sweet older man on a motorized cart pull up. He seemed feeble and unable to take the step up to the ATM, so I offered him help. He said he was all right, so, I just sat in my car in front of the ATM in case he needed assistance.

He stood in front of the ATM, then looked back at me in the car and asked me to come help him. I stepped up. He wanted me to help him withdraw money. He needed to withdraw a couple hundred dollars at a time, over and over. We did just that. He said he needed over $1,000 to get his golf cart back on the road. It had just been repaired.

When he was done, he asked me to help him count the hundred-dollar bills to see what he had. I had him sit in the passenger seat of my car. He laid this stack of bills on my lap and I began counting. I guess I must have looked trustworthy. After I completed counting and handed the money back to him, I encouraged him to put it in a deep pocket.

We talked about his bad health. I asked if he knew about Jesus. He wanted to know, so we prayed together. He became a child of God right then and there in my car. I realized that he must live close by since he was on a motorized scooter, and he did.

Actually, I learned he lived in the same 55-and-older community I lived in. Only God could have done this.

The next day, I wanted to go by his place to drop off a picture that I often share of Jesus holding a lamb in His nail pierced hands. As I was driving there, he passed me. I stopped and asked him if he remembered who I was. He said, "Yes! You're the Jesus Lady."

I have never felt so unworthy. I am humbled beyond words to be called by His name. I am only what my Lord calls me to be. May we all seek to be called Jesus' people!

Anthony

My husband had been keeping his ears open to see if he could find an inexpensive golf cart. One day, a friend stopped by our place to tell us that he knew of a man who had a fixer-upper golf cart that he was looking to sell for a good price. We got the address and were off with the money in hand.

It seems that Anthony had bought this golf cart intending to fix it up for himself. He was a mechanic by trade, but he had had a stroke and knew he could no longer get down and do the work. His plans drastically changed.

It helped him to get the $200 for the cart, and it helped us to only pay that much for it. Paul, too, is a mechanic, so these two men really hit it off.

Anthony even had a trailer that could be used to move the cart from his place to ours. After we managed to push the golf cart up on the trailer, we all sat on his patio to have a drink of water.

I asked Anthony if – now that his health had taken a turn for the worse – he knew when he passed away that he'd go to Heaven.

He replied, "Oh, no! I'm sure I'd go to hell. That's where all my friends will be. I'm too bad to go to Heaven. I wouldn't know anybody there."

I asked Paul to go to the car and bring a Bible tract from my door. I read it to Anthony, then we prayed for him to accept Christ and become a child of God.

The smile and change in that man was remarkable. He was going to know at least two people when we all get to Heaven. Well, he'll know Jesus who gave his life for him. We will just be there also.

If we are listening to God's still small voice and his prompting, He will lead us to one person after another. There is a hurt and dying world out there just waiting to learn about Jesus Christ. May we never be weary in well-doing.

John 4:35: Lift up your eyes, and look on the fields; for they are white already unto harvest.

What's Next?

In 1999, God allowed me to experience His presence in such a mighty, powerful way. Let me back up to the very beginning. My husband had a business going to flea markets. He would purchase products that would then be delivered by UPS. We would just put a money order in an envelope on our front door for the supplier, and the UPS driver would take the money order and leave the order on our doorstep.

One day, I received a phone call from our daughter while I was at work. She was concerned because there was an empty envelope blowing in the wind on our door. There were also no products on our doorstep.

It appeared that the wind had blown the envelope upside down and the money orders had blown away. Since the money orders couldn't be for more than $300, we had put in two money orders. One was for $300. The other was for $55.02. Neither was to be found.

I asked her to walk around our property to see if she could see either of them. We lived in the country. Farmers' fields were all around us. After quite a while, she called to say that she had found the larger one but the smaller one was gone. We ran to get another one to replace the $55.02 order, so that our delivery could still be dropped off. We just had to "eat" the lost $55.02.

About a month after that windy day, I got a visit from my daughter and daughter-in-law. They sat at my kitchen table to share some crushing news with me. An article in the local newspaper caused me to have a total breakdown.

As I was crying at the table, they reminded me that my grandchildren were in the other room playing and we should probably go around back to continue talking. They left to walk around the house to the picnic tables in the back yard. I went to the bathroom to wash my face.

I also needed time to beg God to show me that He was with me. I wanted to trust His hand in my life but I was scared to death. Only He could pull me through. I felt so weak and alone.

Then, God appeared. As I went out my front door and walked the exact path that my daughter and daughter-in-law had taken to the picnic tables in back. I saw the hand of God. In the grass, right where they had just walked, was the missing money order. It wasn't stuck in the siding of the house or in a tree or bush. It was just lying in the grass ahead of my next step.

It had been missing for so long. It was not just by chance that it was in front of me now. My sweet Lord had purposely laid it right there as proof of His presence. I cried tears of comfort and relief.

He was bigger than any problem that I could foresee. He was my strength and my shield, my ever-present help in trouble. I no longer had any doubt that this trial was for His glory and that I was going to make it out just fine.

By the way, the company to which the money order was made out was: What's Next Mfg.! That, too, was a wonderful touch from God. What's next really? Was it too big for my Lord and me to handle? Surely not!

The next day at work, that sweet money order got laminated and I keep it handy everywhere I go. Having a keepsake from various times that the Lord has touched my life is so important to me.

Accident

For many years, my husband and I have enjoyed riding on a fully-dressed Harley Davidson. I just learned how much fun that was in my 50s. After work or on Saturdays, we would hop on and enjoy a ride.

The pastor of our church rode a Harley, as well. We had a group of bikers from our church who would plan trips every now and then on a Saturday. It was great fun.

One particular Saturday was totally different. It was a beautiful, sunny day. As I was riding on the back of our bike, I was just talking to the Lord. That was the way I usually traveled. It was uninterrupted time with Him. I was thanking Him for the beautiful day, saying I felt such a peace that I could handle anything that might come my way. Then it did!

There were probably 12 bikes that day. About four of us in the middle of the line began to slide and roll because of something slick on the road. First the pastor went down, then the next two, followed by our bike. One minute, I was on the back of the bike with my hands comfortably resting on Paul's shoulders. The next second, I was up in the air about to hit the blacktop.

The bikers behind us say they heard me say (quite loudly), "Oh, no!"

The next thing I knew I was looking at the road coming up to my face. I was at the complete mercy of my God. I slid face first until I stopped. The next thing I was aware of was my husband above me, asking me if I was all right. My head was bleeding and I hurt. He had been thrown and slid but was able to crawl over to me.

Ambulances came and took riders to a local hospital to be checked out. Because I was the only one bleeding, I was sent the Hershey Medical Center. They explained that anyone bleeding couldn't just go to a local hospital, in case there might be an undetected head injury.

They sent me for a full body CAT scan. We waited for the results. When the results came back, the doctor said he had some good news and some bad news. First, he said the good news was that I had no broken bones. Praise God. The bad news was that the CAT scan showed something very deep in my one breast that would need to be looked into.

I went to an oncologist who could not find anything with a mammogram nor an ultrasound. She could only see it on the CAT scan. A needle biopsy and then a core biopsy were done in order to remove an area that would have probably become cancer if left alone. God chose to allow me to have the accident to reveal to me a hidden problem.

Then, I shared with the pastor what God had revealed to me. The accident was just so I could be made aware of this deep problem. I said I was so sorry that they all had to be hurt because of me.

I'll never forget his classic words. "It's OK, Jan. We would have taken the fall for you any day."

What a terrific Christian body of believers and reflections of Christ they are. Christ took the fall for each and every one of us. Praise His holy name.

Another keepsake that hangs in my bedroom is pair of sunglasses that I wore on that day. On the right side of the glasses are deep scratches covering the entire lens. The glasses were ruined but not a scratch was on my face. My bleeding was the result of the sun visor coming off of my helmet. God's hand covered me completely. He never let go of me for a second.

Closing

My sister, Kitty, pointed out to me a habit I have when around strangers for the first time. It has to be something that God began in me after I first became His. With the confidence that was only a part of me when He made me know how totally loved I was, I began to do this.

For instance, when going into our recreation center swimming pool for water aerobics for the first time, she watched me approach women like this: "Hi. I'm Jan and you are?"

She thought that was really strange. How was I ever going to remember all those names? So, after we left, she asked me why I do that. My answer: "So that I can pray for them."

Next time I see them, they may or may not remember my name. That doesn't matter. What matters is that I appear friendly. So, the next time I see them and ask how they are, they may share with me a concern that I can pray with them about. It's all about Him—definitely not me.

May He continually be glorified by the life He's given me.